THE MAKING OF A MAVERICK MISSIONARY

Published by
Luviri Press
P/Bag 201, Luwinga, Mzuzu

ISBN 978-99960-968-4-6
A Luviri Monograph

Luviri Press is represented outside Africa by:
African Books Collective Oxford (orders@africanbookscollective.com)

www.luviripress.blogpost.com
www.africanbookscollective.com

Cover Design: Dorothee Marks

Cover Picture: Melbourne Wharf

THE MAKING OF A MAVERICK MISSIONARY
JOSEPH BOOTH AUSTRALASIA

KLAUS FIEDLER

LUVIRI PRESS
MZUZU
2016

Contents

1. The Maverick Missionary

Introduction

No one who reads the history of Malawi can bypass the name of Joseph Booth. If it was not him who coined the slogan "Africa for the African", he was definitely one of those who used it early and regularly and did much to propagate it. He even wrote a book with that title,[1] and he was not even a black American, but just an ordinary white man. Though he was white indeed, he may not have been so ordinary and like the rest of them, after all.

500 Malawi Kwacha showing Chilembwe's portrait

And anyone who wants to learn about John Chilembwe, Malawi's national hero, will never understand him, unless he understands Joseph Booth, too. Without Booth John Chilembwe would never have gone to the United States, returning from there in 1900 as a missionary of the National [Black American] Baptist Convention Inc.[2]

Without Booth taking him to America, the Chilembwe uprising of 1915

---

[1]   Joseph Booth, *Africa for the African*, Baltimore: Morgan College Press, 1897; reprinted Blantyre: CLAIM-Kachere, 1998 (ed. Laura Perry) and Zomba: Kachere, 2008. The reprint reproduces the second edition of 1897, with a critical apparatus comparing it to the first edition, and explanatory footnotes.

[2]   The Inc. behind the name is important, as there is another National Baptist Convention of America, distinguishing itself from its sister by the lack of "Inc." – For the NBC missionary work in Malawi see: Patrick Makondesa, *The Church History of Providence Industrial Mission*, Zomba: Kachere, 2006.

would not have taken place, but then, Joseph Booth was a pacifist, and how come that he "caused" an armed uprising?[3]

Much has been written about Joseph Booth, foremost the excellent biography written by his great-grandson, Harry Langworthy,[4] and before him George Shepperson's *Independent African*, which deals with John Chilembwe but of necessity includes much on Joseph Booth.[5] Authors differ in their evaluation of Booth, seeing in him everything from saint to scoundrel, and anything between a fool and an illusionist, and maybe a man ahead of his time or out of tune with it. This book is not to attempt such an evaluation,[6] but it tries to answer one question: "What made Joseph Booth to become the maverick missionary that he did become?"

Several ideas have been proposed: The most ingenious is "Sure, he was a Black American".[7] Though he had many sympathies and much admiration for them, his skin was white and he was born in England, not in America. Another idea, less imaginative but probably also off track, is: "Maybe because of his working class background". At that time almost everyone had a working class background somewhere,

---

[3] For an account of the Rising see: D.D. Phiri, *Let us Die for Africa,* Blantyre: 2000. For a play on the Rising see: D.D. Phiri, *Let us Fight for Africa*, Zomba: Kachere, 2007. Phiri deals with this question by making Chilembwe meet Joseph Booth at the River Mbombwe on the eve of the Rising in what turns out to have been a dream (p. 67-70). In reality Booth knew nothing of the Rising until he was deported from Lesotho and South Africa for supporting it.

[4] Harry Langworthy, *"Africa for the African". The Life of Joseph Booth*, Blantyre: CLAIM-Kachere, 1996.

[5] George Shepperson and Tom Price, *Independent African. John Chilembwe and the Nyasaland Rising of 1915*, Blantyre: CLAIM-Kachere [6]2000 (first edition Edinburgh University Press 1958).

[6] For my attempt on that see: Klaus Fiedler, "Joseph Booth and the Writing of Malawian History. An Attempt at Interpretation'" *Religion in Malawi* no. 6, 1996, pp. 30-38.

[7] Jeff Hayes, *Religion in Third World Politics*, Oxford: Blackwell, 1994.

somewhen, but he came to Malawi after having sold his business in Melbourne. He was probably not rich, but that sale paid for his and his two children's tickets from Australia to London and from there to Africa,[8] and there was money left in the bank to be sent to him at quarterly intervals.

I am not sure if I can give a conclusive answer. But what I did was to fill the gap, maybe the answer would be there. Harry Langworthy's biography of 520 pages, which is full of details and deep understanding, only devotes six pages to the ten years in Auckland and Melbourne. The reason is simple: The author never had a chance to go there. Here I was luckier: When my youngest daughter got married in Hobart, Tasmania, I took a week to follow the Booths to Melbourne, trying to find out who they were there before Joseph Booth and the children came here. And four years later I did the same for Auckland, extending my second visit to my Hobart daughter.

I did find the Booths in both places. I was fascinated to see the house which they built in Auckland (again not a sign of working class status),[9] to worship in Auckland Tabernacle, of which they were members more than a century ago, and to read the archives of Brighton Baptist Church in Melbourne, to which they belonged. And I was intrigued by the difficulties I had in finding the famous "Hall of Science" where he, the ex-atheist, debated with Joseph Symes, the ex-Christian. The Hall of Science was probably less than a quarter of the size it had in Emily Booth's memory, but it was fascinating to read the Atheist *Liberator* and to realize that, if Joseph Booth was a somewhat difficult character, his opponent in debate was ten times that.

Did I find the answer: "Why did he become the maverick he eventually became?" Maybe not, since it is easier to ask such a question than to answer it. But I found his background, from which he grew to be the person he became. He was a Baptist and that with a special "Tabernacle" touch. Since there were a few thousand Baptists of that type in Australasia,[10] this must not have *caused* him to become the maverick he became, but he used that background to develop into the odd man out, and though he clashed with many contemporary ideas, he never broke nor clashed with the background that formed him. Joseph Booth

---

[8]   He had also purchased the ticket for his wife Mary Jane, but she died three weeks before departure.

[9]   I also learned that they never owned a sheep farm and probably never set a foot on one of them.

[10]   Australasia is a term, then and now, being used to cover New Zealand and Australia.

was not a politician, but a missionary, and he was not a social reformer, but a Baptist. But as a Baptist he did become a social reformer and a politician, with all his motivation on the religious side. For him it was "Africa for Christ", and to that "Africa for the African" was a necessary corollary.

The early years in Britain

My story of Booth begins in Auckland, 1879. Up to then I follow Harry Langworthy:[11] Joseph Booth was born in Derby in 1851, with a Unitarian father and an Anglican mother. The national feelings of his extended family (at least of the male members) did not stop him from becoming a pacifist (and that he remained all his life long) and neither did his somewhat religious upbringing stop him from becoming an atheist (which he remained only a few years).

He started his journey back to the Christian faith when he began to realize that the atheists and agnostics he loved to read and to hear might have overstated their case.[12] That he fell in love with Mary Jane Sharp, a Baptist girl with a living faith, helped to draw him closer to an equal commitment, which he confirmed through his baptism in Rotherham Baptist Church in 1872, not long before their wedding.

2. The Booths in Auckland

Joseph Booth had started his working life at the age of 15 as a booking clerk at Buxton, Derbyshire, moved to commercial clerk in Rotherham in 1872 and to dairyman in Sheffield in 1875.[13] If he had not left the working class already in Sheffield, he did so when the Booths (with their son Edward) migrated to New Zealand, ostensibly to find a climate more suited to Mary Jane's "week lungs". If they travelled to Auckland with an emigration subsidy or if they took their own money with them is not known. But they left determined and with energy to build up a new life in a new country. They arrived in New Zealand when immigrants were highly welcome. From 1871 till 1880 New Zealand received about 100,000 immigrants, whose fares were often partly or fully paid by the government.[14] Jobs were plentiful and investors were eager. This

---

[11] Harry Langworthy, *"Africa for the African". The Life of Joseph Booth*, pp. 17-21.

[12] In Melbourne he would come across such overstatements again.

[13] It is not clear if he was in that profession as an employee or running his own shop.

[14] Within ten years, the European population almost doubled, growing from 256,393 in 1871 to 489,933 in 1881 (Keith Sinclair [ed.], *The Oxford Illustrated History of New Zealand*, Auckland: OUP, 1993 [1990], p. 104).

applied to all of New Zealand, but in Auckland there was a special boom, based on land.

In Auckland, the Booths found a thriving and growing city in its best mood of colonial expansion. The beginnings of the city as a colonial settlement date back to the 1840s, when European settlers started to replace the Maori population of the area around the Bay of Islands.[15] After the New Zealand wars of 1860 to 1872, what had been a pioneer settlement grew into the leading town of the North Island,[16] being surrounded by smaller settlements.[17]

When the Booths came in 1880, the core of the city was already quite well built up[18] with Queen Street as the main street. Queen Street issued into the Waitemata harbour area, where the steam ferries from across the Bay would land.[19] Auckland was the centre of administration for the North Island and was leading in business, which had trade with Britain as its major foreign supply line.[20] The Booths were strictly speaking not citizens of this city,[21] but of Waitemata, across the Bay, or the

---

[15] On July 29, 1841, a group of Maori chiefs, including Apihai te Kawau, Tinana, and Reweti Tamaki, sold about 1,214 hectares to the government. The price was 50 pounds sterling, 50 blankets, 20 trousers, 20 shirts, 10 waistcoats, 10 caps, 4 casks of tobacco, 1 box of pipes, 91 metres of gown pieces, 10 iron pots, 1 bag of sugar, 1 bag of flour, and 20 hatchets. The first two ships of migrants for Auckland—the Duchess of Argyle and the Jane Gifford—arrived from Greenock, in Scotland, on Oct. 9, 1842, carrying 535 settlers ("Auckland", *World Book Millennium 2000*, International Standard English Edition, Version 4.0, IBM, CD ROM).

[16] From 1841 to 1881 its population had grown to 16,664, until 1886 it doubled with 33,161 (John Barr, *The City of Auckland, New Zealand, 1840-1920*, Auckland et al: Whitcombe and Tombs, 1922. In 1871 Auckland was made a city.

[17] One such settlement was Howick, which was settled by Fencibles, the soldier–settlers who defended Auckland against possible Maori attacks, in 1847. It has the oldest New Zealand church building still in use. For the history of church and parish see: Robert Hattaway and Margaret Willis, *When all the Saints. Celebrating 150 Years of All Saints' Church – Howick*, Auckland: Howick Parish, 1997. For the early history see Robert Hattaway's article pp. 26 ff. - I am grateful to Revs. Dianne and Bruce Miller-Keeley, the present Vicars of All Saints, for graciously accepting me into their house and hearts during my research in Auckland.

[18] G.W.A. Bush, *Decently and in Order. The Centennial History of the Auckland City Council*, Auckland/London: Collins, 1971, p. 115.

[19] Steam ferries, then, were an important means of transport as are the catamaran ferries now, with a new ferry along the coast to Howick competing effectively against the bus services (from Monday to Friday).

[20] The major economic event of these years was the introduction of refrigerated ships which could take meat and butter to Britain.

[21] This is true from 1882 onwards, possibly they lived before that in the city itself, but I could not find any evidence, as Booth is not recorded in the contemporary "Voters' Roll".

North Shore, as it was popularly known then and now. In this growing and exciting colonial city Mary Jane and Joseph Booth (with their son Edward, born 1876) made their new home, and there their daughter Emily was born 4 August 1884.[22] Joseph Booth continued in his occupation as a dairy man, and must have done well since they were able to buy two plots on the North shore in what is today Devonport[23] and to build a house on plot no. 31.[24] Devonport started as a suburban settlement outside Auckland in the 1860s,[25] was by then developing into an upcoming suburb,[26] not for the poor of the city.[27] The Booths' address was corner of Cheltenham Place and William Street,[28] located in an area being newly developed about 15 minutes from a nice beach on the far side of Devonport and about 15 minutes from Devonport centre[29] and the landing of the steam ferry to Auckland.[30]

Their housing area was located between Mt. Victoria (Taka a Ranga) in the west (excellent view over the Bay) and North Head (Maungauika) with military fortifications against seaborne Russian attacks.[31]

---

[22] Harry Langworthy, *"Africa for the African". The Life of Joseph Booth*, Blantyre: CLAIM-Kachere, 1996, p. 22.

[23] In 1882 there were 220 buildings in Devonport, 492 in 1888.

[24] Built with a mortgage from the Industrial and Provident Permanent Building and Investment Society, entered on 27.11.1882 (Certificate of Title, Vol 15, Freio 281 (13 A.540), Lands Office, Auckland.)

[25] There had been some houses even in the 1850s and up to the end of the 1870s growth had been slow. 1880 – 1887 was a period of rapid growth, followed by some decline (Susan Sheehan, "A Social and Demographic Study of Devonport, 1850-1920," MA, University of Auckland, 1980, p. 29).

[26] See T. Walsh, *An Illustrated Story of Devonport and the Old North Shore 1841 to 1924, with an Outline of Maori Occupation to 1841*; Auckland, nd.; S. Musgrove (ed.), *The Hundred of Devonport. A Centennial History*, Devonport: Borough Council, nd.

[27] The population doubled from 1881 to 1886, from 1319 to 2650 (Susan Sheehan, "A Social and Demographic Study of Devonport, 1850-1920," MA, University of Auckland, 1980, p. 21).

[28] Today Oxford Terrace 11 (with the old house) and 9 with a house built later.

[29] Only in 1888 was a horse tram line built from Cheltenham to Duder's Corner (T. Walsh, *An Illustrated Story of Devonport and the Old North Shore 1841 to 1924, with an Outline of Maori Occupation to 1841*; Auckland, nd., p. 31).

[30] The steam ferry had started running in 1881, every 30 minutes up to 11 pm (Susan Sheehan, "A Social and Demographic Study of Devonport, 1850-1920," MA, University of Auckland, 1980, p. 29).

[31] During the Russian scare 1884-1886 four 64 pounds Howitzer guns were installed. The Russians had no intention to scare New Zealand; the guns were never used and serve the tourist trade today. It can be safely concluded that Joseph Booth, the pacifist, was not favourably impressed by them and all that was going on around them.

View of Auckland City from Devonport

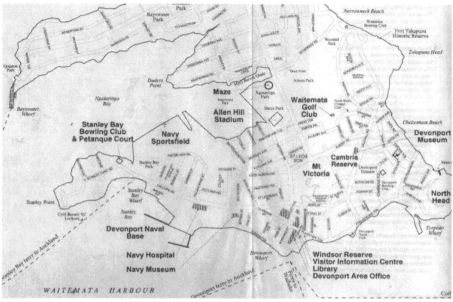

Map of Devonport

From the records available to me I could not find any details on Joseph Booth's workplace. In the Voters' Register of 1882 he is a dairy man, and since he was that in Sheffield in England before coming to New Zealand and since he later owned a "milk palace" in Melbourne, there is little reason to doubt that that was his occupation in Auckland as well. "Dairy man" can mean three things in New Zealand: (1) an employee in or owner of a rural dairy where milk products are produced. (2) The owner of a store that supplies milk and milk products, often by delivering to the people where they live in regular tours. (3) The owner of a general shop (in other countries called grocery), which sells milk and milk products among other things. Since Booth was a city dweller, he was most probably not a producer of dairy products[32] but a supplier. Since in Melbourne he was a specialized dairy man, it may be easiest to imagine him to have been a milk products supplier in Auckland, too.

It would be nice to find out if he worked in Devonport, where his house was, or across the bay in Auckland city where there were far more people than in little Devonport, but I found no evidence either way.[33]

Auckland Baptist Church

Though I could not find evidence of his workplace, there is plenty on their church, and that was always in Auckland City. In those years in Devonport there were an Anglican church, a Catholic church, a Methodist church and a Presbyterian church.[34] But the Booths had been Baptists in England already, so they joined the only Baptist congregation then existing in the Auckland area, Wellesley Street Baptist Church, and most probably their son Edward did not attend the Catholic school in Devonport but the government school.[35]

Wellesley Street was the third oldest Baptist congregation in New Zealand, and the first on the North Island.[36] It was started in 1855 by 13 members led by James Thornton, who became their first pastor.[37]

---

[32] There is no support for the idea that he was a sheep farmer in New Zealand as assumed in George Shepperson and Tom Price, *Independent African. John Chilembwe and the Nyasaland Rising of 1915*, Blantyre: CLAIM-Kachere [6]2000, p. 21.

[33] The Booths' house, as it stands now, certainly does not show any sign that it was ever built for or used as business premises. I am grateful to Mr Colin Watt of 9 Oxford Terrace for showing me around.

[34] The 1891 figures of members counted by denominations allow a conclusion on the religious composition of the Devonport population even in the Booths' time: Anglican 1169 (48%), Presbyterian 358 (15%), Methodist 320 (13%), Roman Catholic 186 (8%).

[35] *Devonport District School Centennial Publication 1870-1970*, nd., np. In 1882 the school had five teachers including the Head Teacher. In 1884 Alfred Benge was Head Master. In 1885 there were 380 pupils. Most teachers were female. See Jacque Sharpe and J. de Joswald, Devonport District School, Historic Committee Papers, 1882-1885 (in Devonport Library).

[36] The first Baptist churches were Nelson (1851) and not far from there, Richmond, in the same year (*A Sunday School's Half Century, 1858-1908*).

[37] James Thornton - Charles Haddon Spurgeon 1861. In 1858 a church for 300 people was built on freehold land.

Rev P.H. Cornford took over in 1862,[38] and in 1884 the church building was enlarged to 500 seats.[39] Due to its size and good situation[40] it had become a reputable city church.

Wellesley Street Baptist Church felt not only responsible for the city, but also for the surrounding area, and new churches were started at Thames (1869), Mt. Eden (1886) and Ponsonby (1880),[41] and Baptist church work was also carried on at Otahuhu[42] and Cambridge.

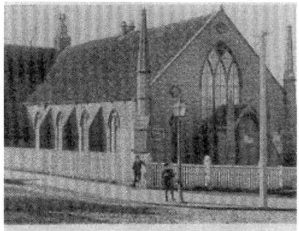

Wellesley Street Baptist Church

In 1877 Rev Allan Webb became the pastor of Auckland Baptist Church, and when Mary Jane and Joseph Booth transferred their membership in 1880,[43] they found an active church, thriving both on

---

[38] He had been a missionary of the Baptist Missionary Society in Jamaica for 10 years.

[39] It is possible that Charles H. Spurgeon of the Metropolitan Tabernacle in London gave some financial assistance.

[40] The church was originally located at the corner of Wellesley and Federal Street. The property was sold and later demolished. Today the ASB Bank Tower stands on the plot, and a plaque commemorates Wellesley Street Baptist Church.

[41] All three places are now suburbs of Auckland. Ponsonby, being closest to the centre, had the privilege of being the end point of Auckland's first (horse drawn) tram line, started on 11.8.1884. The electric tram started running only on 16.11.1902.

[42] "Besides Mt. Eden, the new cause at Otahuhu is prospering" (Minutes Annual meeting of church members, 25.8.1887)

[43] "Letters of dismission to be sent on behalf of Mr and Mrs Booth" (Minutes, Church Meeting of 26.11.1880). To get the letters took some time, on 25.11.1880 "the Pastor intimated the receipt of letters of dismission for ... Mr and Mrs. Booth - on the vote of the members. Mr and Mrs Booth were fully admitted into fellowship (Minutes, Church Meeting

immigration and evangelism, and growing for both reasons.[44] The church was active, and the pastor's positive assessment seems to have been justified.

> 3rd Spiritual Aspect of the Church - He was thankful that the Lord had kept the people - unity was preserved, kindly social intercourse prevailed among the people. The ties between Pastor and people had been strengthened. There were good evidences that our young converts had grown in spiritual life.[45]

The Booths were not young converts anymore, but they too came into a congregation with over 400 members that provided them with a good environment for spiritual growth.[46] The church had two services on a Sunday; there was a strong Sunday School as the "first agency of the church."[47] There was evangelistic work in the form of "open air preaching in the public thoroughfare in Auckland" (only during summer) and in form of tract distribution and personal witness,[48] and care for the poor.[49]

The church was clearly evangelical and evangelistic. Pastor Webb stated that the "conditions for success in the church were (1) Personal religion and (2) Scripturalness of doctrine." He continued, in addressing the members of this congregation:

> Our safety is to carry on our operations from within the old evangelistic lines – of human depravity and ruin and the vicarious suffering of Jesus; and if we are to win souls for Christ, we must use the heavenly attempered and well-tested weapons which the Reformers and Puritans and early Methodists found so effectual.[50]

In this statement Webb combines the contradictions, by claiming both the Calvinistic Puritans and the Arminian Methodists as shining examples. In this he represented many Baptists of his age, who under the influence first of (Arminian) Methodism and then of the (Arminian)

26.5.1881. Though a good number of dismissal letters received are still at the Tabernacle Archive, the Booths' letter is not there.

[44] In 1884 32 new members were received into fellowship by "report and dismissal", and 53 were received "from the world". Nine members died, 8 were "struck off", three were "dismissed to join other churches."

[45] Wellesley Street Baptist Church, Annual Meeting of Church Members, 25.8.1880.

[46] At the end of 1883 the church had 602 members, and the same year 53 had joined through conversion and baptism, and 32 through transfer. The losses were small: 3 transfers to other churches, 9 deaths and 8 members "struck off" (Annual Report 1884).

[47] In 1884 the Sunday School had 400 scholars and 40 teachers (*The Baptist*, 25.7.1884).

[48] *Manual Baptist Church, Wellesley St., Auckland, 1878*, p. 16 ff.

[49] To help the poor there were the "Poor Fund" and the "Comfort Poor Fund" (Ibid.).

[50] *Manual, Baptist Church, Wellesley St., Auckland*, 1878, p.6.

Holiness Revival had learned to *teach* Calvinism and to *behave* as Arminians.[51] This same attitude was shared by Webb's successor in the Wellesley pulpit and by Joseph Booth.

A similar combination of opposites characterized the church's policy towards baptism. Membership depended on believer's baptism ("closed membership"), but communion was "open", and any believer in Christ could be admitted. But if someone did not see the need for believers' baptism, and yet wanted to participate fully in the life of Auckland Baptist Church, she or he could ask to be placed on the role of "communicants".[52] In Auckland Baptist Church "personal religion" took priority over minor points of doctrinal correctness, thus making room for the evangelistic task of the church.

Not all Baptist churches in Britain in those days shared these attitudes, and I know nothing about the attitude of the Booths' church in England, but it is obvious that the Booths were spiritually formed in this context and all his life Joseph Booth held clearly Baptist views *and* the conviction that missionary work had to take precedence over doctrine.[53]

Webb, who received the Booth's in Auckland, did not stay as their pastor for long, as on 13.9.1881 he informed the church that he had accepted a call from North Adelaide Baptist Church, where he had before been working as a "supply pastor" for one month.[54] Next week he explained that one reason for his resignation was that he could not get the deacons to see the need "to obtain a site more suited to a Central City Church".[55]

---

[51] See Klaus Fiedler, *The Story of the Faith Missions*, Oxford: Regnum, [2]1995, pp. 223-224 on the "Arminianization of Calvinism".

[52] In 1880 there were six such "permanent" unbaptized communicants. (*Manual, Baptist Church Wellesley St., Auckland*, 1887, p. 12).

[53] This attitude was also shared by Thomas Spurgeon, who would even baptize believers from other churches without necessarily expecting them to become Baptists. One Thursday, the regular day for baptisms in this church, he baptized four Anglicans and two Methodists who wanted to remain full members of their churches, together with five who would become Baptists, and two who were not yet clear which course to pursue (*The Standard*, Chicago, 25.8.1887).

[54] Pastor Webb's letter was read to the congregation on 14.9.1881, which responded that "It is with deepest regret that the members of this church have heard the letter from our pastor in which he resigns his charge of this church, and that he be requested to reconsider it." An amendment, proposed by two members, "that Mr Webb's resignation be accepted pure and simple" was lost.

[55] There was agreement, though, that Wellesley Street was becoming too small, and when, under his successor, the new church was built on Queen St, it seems to me to have been less central to the existing City, but perhaps more suitable for a growing city (Rev. Webb - Auckland Baptist Church, 20.9.1881).

When Webb resigned, the church had been in contact already with Thomas Spurgeon,[56] who had acted as supply pastor in Auckland while Webb had been acting as supply pastor in Adelaide, and he had impressed both church and City. So it was easy to call him to become their pastor. On 19.10.1881, he accepted provisionally and after having received his parents' consent, definitely on 30.11.1881. Thomas Spurgeon, one of the twin sons and only children of Susanna and Charles Haddon Spurgeon, had a health problem similar to Mary Jane Booth's "weak lungs", and so his parents arranged a trip to Australia and New Zealand, (rightly) expecting that the long sea voyage with its harsh maritime climate would invigorate his health and that the absence of the London smog and the presence of warmer temperatures in Australasia would keep his health in good shape.

Since Charles Haddon Spurgeon was the most famous Protestant preacher of his age,[57] he had many friends in Australia, and since his sermons were published immediately after they were preached,[58] and spread all over the English speaking world, they were even read in the remotest Australian outback,[59] and that added to the many friends he knew a much large number of friends that knew him. Thomas Spurgeon, arriving in Melbourne was, of course, very welcome as his famous father's son, but since his father had dropped a hint in his letter of recommendation—"By the way, he can preach a bit"[60]that was taken up immediately, everybody wanted to hear the son of the great

[56] His biography is: Craig Skinner, *Spurgeon and Son. The Forgotten Story of Thomas Spurgeon and his Famous Father, Charles Haddon Spurgeon*, Grand Rapids: Kregel, 1999. Originally published as *Lamplighter and Son*, Nashville: Broadman, 1984. Pp. 120-156 contain a pictorial record of Thomas Spurgeon's Life in 201 pictures.

[57] For Charles Haddon Spurgeon see: Susannah Spurgeon and Joseph Harald (eds.), *C.H. Spurgeon. Autobiography, Compiled from his Diary, Letters and Records by his Wife and Private Secretary, London 1897-1910*. A two volume abbreviated version, London 1962 and 1973. For a more conservative interpretation see: Iain Murray, *The Forgotten Spurgeon*, London 1966.

[58] Spurgeon, for much of his life, preached to congregations of 5000 to 6000, first in the Crystal Palace, then in the Metropolitan Tabernacle. The sermons were recorded by stenographers, on Monday morning Spurgeon would check them, and then they were telegraphed to America and available for sale on Tuesday. From 1894-1908 Thomas Spurgeon became his fathers' successor (Craig Skinner, *Spurgeon and Son*, pp. 157-191).

[59] Craig Skinner, *Spurgeon and Son*, p. 17 reports of an Australian "swagman", unable to hold a job for long over five years, due to alcohol, who was converted by reading a sermon in a newspaper outside a public house, and led a Christian life, holding a steady job, ever after.

[60] Craig Skinner, *Lamplighter and Son. The Forgotten Story of Thomas Spurgeon and his Famous Father, Charles Haddon Spurgeon*, Nashville: Broadman 1984.

preacher, so wherever he preached the place filled easily.[61] Very soon Thomas Spurgeon as much as his listeners discovered that he had indeed his own gift of preaching, and so he decided not only to travel on his father's ticket but also to preach his way through southern Australia to Tasmania[62] and from there through New Zealand upwards to Auckland.[63] In his preaching he would put much emphasis on evangelism, as that was dear to his heart, and at a time of spiritual quickening in the context of the Holiness Revival,[64] welcome among the congregations that would invite him.

It was in this capacity that Thomas Spurgeon reached Auckland in 1881 and Wellesley Street Baptist Church, as so many other churches had done, was keen to avail itself of his services in evangelism, as anniversary preacher and for the extension of Baptist work.[65] When these things were being arranged, Allen Webb unexpectedly resigned as pastor, so why not call Thomas Spurgeon, whose preaching had found so much acclaim? He had never been to a theological school,[66] neither had he been ordained,[67] but that was no problem in the Baptist set up.

In becoming pastor of Wellesley Street Baptist Church in Auckland, Thomas Spurgeon joined an expanding congregation with a clearly evangelical piety, with its regular evangelical emphasis on personal

---

[61] His first sermon was on the first Sunday evening ashore in Rev Bunning's New Baptist Church in Aberdeen Street in Geelong, when 900 persons crowded the sanctuary that normally would hold a maximum of 700. Rev Bunning was one of the students at Spurgeon's Pastors' College. (Craig Skinner, *Spurgeon and Son*, pp. 22-24).

[62] There he saw for the first time Lila Rutherford, then aged 13, who would become his wife in February 1888, Thomas F. Hill, "History of the Auckland Bapt. Tabernacle", *The Reaper*, 1924-26, p. 15, (a copy in the Tabernacle Archives)

[63] Minutes Wellesley Street Baptist Church 5.1.1881 and 3.8.1881.

[64] For the Holiness Revival (others call it the Second Evangelical Awakening) and its effects on missions see: Klaus Fiedler, *The Story of Faith Missions from Hudson Taylor to Present Day Africa*, Oxford et al.: Regnum, ²1995, pp. 112-124.

[65] Minutes Wellesley Street Baptist Church 24.8.1881 for preaching, 28.9.1881 for helping in the establishment of Cambridge Baptist Church.

[66] Minutes Monthly Church Meeting January 1882.

[67] In Auckland Spurgeon was of course the Rev Spurgeon. But the church minutes give no hint of any ordination, nor that he had received any formal training in theology, which would be in line with Baptist principles of biblical interpretation and with his father's spirit, who also was never ordained and never attended theological college, though he later founded one. – Thomas Spurgeon himself claimed to have been ordained by the Australian Steam Navigation Co., whose clerk decided that he could get a reduced fare for signing his name as "Rev.", though he was not even wearing the "required white tie" (Craig Skinner, *Spurgeon and Son*, p. 43).

faith (very directly related to the bible), evangelism and missions and applied Christianity expressed in concern for the poor and the oppressed in society.[68] All this he shared with his predecessor, so he continued an existing development of outreach and growth, a structure that the Booths had found in place when they joined the congregation. To what he found he added the charm of his personality and his unusual gift of public delivery in general and preaching in particular.

Mrs Thomas Spurgeon (Nee Lila Rutherford)

Not the least of Thomas Spurgeon's attractions was his humour. He was even applauded "for a racy and humorous speech",[69] and his sermons were lively (and often with a good laugh). Even in print jokes were welcome.

> Instructor in Latin — "Miss B., of what was Ceres the goddess?" — Miss B. —"She was the goddess of marriage." — Instructor sharply — "Oh, no – of agriculture!" Miss B., looking perplexed — "Why, I am sure my book says she was the goddess of husbandry!"[70]

This attitude, that the Holy Spirit liked jokes and fresh air, Thomas Spurgeon must have learnt from his father. His humour was occasionally paid back in kind by friendly observers. On the occasion of his trip to London in 1885, the *Daily Telegraph* commented:

> Mr. Spurgeon has lived down much opposition and prejudice in Auckland, he has advanced the Baptist cause considerably, and established

---

68 Wellesley Street had a Poor Fund, and money from it was invested in the Tabernacle Trust Fund, which still owns a set of offices and shops on Karangahape St. adjacent to the Tabernacle. The Benevolent Society of the church had 62 members in 1887 (32nd Annual Report). In 1884 there was a mission school with 50 boys and girls of the "larrikin class". Some of the boys were "as completely heathen as any savages on the face of the earth."
69 *New Zealand Baptist* 1881.
70 Thomas Spurgeon (ed.), *The Baptist Builder*, Published at the Auckland Tabernacle Bazaar, vol. 1, Dec. 1882.

himself as a popular preacher. I cordially wish him bon voyage, protection from designing mothers on the other side of the herring pond, a
pleasant holiday and a speedy return.[71]

When finally Thomas Spurgeon got married to Lila Rutherford, the
commentator wrote:

> The marriageable maidens of the Baptist Church, ranging from blushing
> 16 to simpering 60, after being kept on the tenter-hooks of matrimonial
> expectancy for two whole years, have been suddenly hurled into the
> abyss of despair.

While the church had already been feeling the need to expand the seating capacity beyond the current 500,[72] and was looking for a potentially
better location, that became now a paramount concern.[73] For the evening services, which would attract a good number of listeners from
other churches, the Choral Hall was hired.[74] Thomas Spurgeon had
become a main attraction for religious people in Auckland.

Thomas Spurgeon, also without much fuss, began to mould the congregation in his ways. The idea to build a bigger church was not new,
but he made sure it would not be called after the street in which it was
built, but "New Zealand Baptist Tabernacle." He also made sure it
would look neither like a chapel (a kind of downsized church with no
tower)[75] nor like a church (gothic in style with a tower and a peal of
bells), but like an attractive public building (for which Doric style would
be quite acceptable).[76] It was also to have several rooms for classes

---

[71] *The Daily Telegraph*, 28.7.1884.

[72] Pastor Allan Web asked the Annual Meeting of Church Members to keep up their
subscription to the New Church Building Fund, as the time was close at hand when
something definite would have to be done in this matter.

[73] Thomas Spurgeon became pastor in November 1881, within one year the congregation
had 108 additions, with 411 members in July 1882 (Circular letter 21.7.1882). On 25.1.1882,
the deacons recommended that the present site of the Tabernacle be purchased for 3200
£ (minutes 25.1.1882)

[74] A sermon which Spurgeon preached there before being appointed pastor of Wellesley
Street is reported like this "Mr Spurgeon preached in the Choral Hall, to a good audience,
on the 4th inst. When first in the pulpit, Mr Spurgeon seems quite juvenile; but from the
moment he commences the service his juvenility is gone, and we listen to one who knows
what he uttereth. The gifts peculiar to a fluent speaker Mr. Spurgeon possesses in no small
degree, whilst he feels persuaded he is possessed of the essential graces (*New Zealand
Baptist*, Sep. 1881).

[75] Wellesley Street Baptist Church was quite a dignified church building, but it looked a bit
like a chapel.

[76] This style was a common feature. The oldest Baptist Church in Hobart, called Tabernacle and built as such, even today shows the origin. Different from Auckland, it had pews

and groups, so as to accommodate a rich and diverse congregational life.

The proposed Tabernacle[77] would be similar to the Metropolitan Tabernacle in London, though its seating capacity would not be around 6000 but above 1200. Still, style and purpose would be similar. The church would be properly heated, the pulpit would be a platform with space for a number of people,[78] chairs would be installed (not pews), and the auditorium would in a way be seated around the platform, which would be achieved by seating many people on a gallery at the back and left side of the auditorium.[79]

---

instead of chairs, but these were curved to create the feeling of a circle, the only curved pews I have ever seen. For the galleries technical devices were installed, but they were never built. – The oldest Tabernacle type church in New Zealand is Cambridge, built for a new church of 40 members, in Doric style, opened 29.4.1883 (*New Zealand Baptist*, June 1883). For Charles Haddon Spurgeon's strong influence in Tasmania see Craig Skinner, *Spurgeon and Son*, pp. 42f and 52.

[77] The term "Tabernacle" is taken from the Old Testament people of God in the wilderness, when God's presence moved with them in the Tent of Meeting. The idea of a Tabernacle church is that the church will go where the people are (often in the new industrial suburbs), not that the people must go where the churches are (often in the old inner cities).

[78] Charles Haddon Spurgeon also liked to use the platform for little demonstrations, as he was a lively speaker. Once he used it to demonstrate the difference (or perceived difference) between the Tabernacle people and other Christians. During a lecture his son gave on New Zealand there was a break, which he used to make things clear: He made some laughable remarks about being able to distinguish the people going to the Metropolitan Tabernacle on Sunday morning from those going to the other places of worship, illustrating by imitation in a walk around the platform the styles of the two classes of people – the one brisk and lively, and the other solemnly slow. The remaining portion of the Thomas Spurgeon's lecture dealt with emigration and the Maoris (*Daily Chronicle*, 15.10.1884).

[79] No listener would be more than 50 feet away from the pulpit.

All these features, equally found in the London Metropolitan Tabernacle, had a major theological significance. The church was to be participatory, it was centred on lively preaching, it was a good and warm place to be in, it had shed the dust of the centuries and the solemnity of a middle and upper class for whom to go to church, weddings and funerals was a duty, though not necessarily a pleasant one. To simplify a bit, the Tabernacle was to be a modern place, designed to proclaim the old, old gospel story to a new and modern generation.[80]

New Zealand Baptist Tabernacle, Auckland

This was in no way a break with the earlier history of Wellesley Street, but neither was it the same thing. The Tabernacle Baptists were regular Baptists, but having said that they were also a new (and innovative) group of their own,[81] centered around "Spurgeon and his men,"[82] those that were trained in his pastor's college and shared his concern for evangelism, social commitment and innovation. They would go to

---

[80] Charles Haddon Spurgeon and his colleagues, both lay and clerical, were unashamedly conservative in their biblical interpretation at a time when many thought that liberal theology was the requirement of the day, and they were unashamedly modern in expressing this old story in words and actions.

[81] This was also expressed in other ways. A letter of dismissal from West London Tabernacle to Auckland Tabernacle mentions nowhere that they were both Baptist. It originates from "The Church of Christ Worshipping in the West London Tabernacle, St. James Square, Notting Hill, W" written for John Hewitt, 12.8.1885.

[82] Paul Tomson, *A Handful of Grain*, p. 29, describes them as giving new impetus to Baptist work, but does not ascribe any peculiar piety or policy to them.

preach where the growing masses of the people were,[83] and where the people were they would establish God's presence, just as God's presence was established wherever his wandering nation of Israel went, through his Tabernacle. As times moved on, God would move on with them, not by accommodating Himself to them, but by establishing his presence in a changing society.

This change from a regular Baptist Church to a Tabernacle Baptist Church took place without a visible struggle, as it was not contrary to the previous history of the Auckland Baptists, and as a successful leader was there to see it through. Just as his father, Thomas Spurgeon also decided that the Tabernacle should be opened free of debt.[84] This was achieved,[85] with the last 1000£ subscribed on opening day.[86] The strong connection between the two Tabernacles[87] is shown in the fact that over £ 2,500 of the total cost of £ 14,628 was contributed by the Metropolitan Tabernacle or paid from collections Thomas Spurgeon was given during his visit to London in 1885,[88] where he also preached for his father several times.[89]

---

[83] That is why the Metropolitan Tabernacle was built on the other side of the River Thames, in line with the industrial growth of the ancient metropolis. Since Auckland was such a new city, such considerations may have played no role there.

[84] There may be well a connection here to the Faith Mission Movement, for which Hudson Taylor expressed the financial concept as: "God's work, done in God's way, will not lack God's supply". The Tabernacle Baptists saw nothing wrong in principle in borrowing money for a new building for worship, but often felt led not to incur debts.

[85] For the sermon, see: Thomas Spurgeon, *Auckland Tabernacle Opening Sermon*, (verbatim reported), Auckland: Theo Cooper, 1885, 18 pp.

[86] Craig Skinner, *Spurgeon and Son*, p. 89. While the Auckland Baptist Tabernacle was indeed opened free of debt, the general fund of the congregation had run into a deficit, which was covered by a loan (minutes 23.11.1885).

[87] This close connection was shown in other ways too. During Thomas Spurgeon's 1884/85 visit to England, C.H. Spurgeon sent W.R. Rice as an interim pastor to replace his son in Auckland, paying his fare to get there. When Thomas Spurgeon left the Tabernacle in November 1889 to become a travelling evangelist for all of New Zealand, his successor was William Birch, again trained and recommended by his father. He was "well known as a popular preacher to the masses." Birch was not a success, he was considered as too liberal (that is how the Baptist papers of Victoria rate him) or too much involved with social and political issues. Thomas Spurgeon left New Zealand in 1892 for England, where he eventually became his father's successor.

[88] The Auckland Tabernacle Building Committee also asked Thomas Spurgeon to thank his father in 1885 for 2537£ 14s 7d contributed in response to a call in *Sword and Trowel*, Charles Haddon Spurgeon's own journal.

[89] His father published his sermon there; Thomas Spurgeon, *The Gospel of the Grace of God*, London: Passmore, 1883.

With this money and their vision, the Auckland Baptists built what became the largest and most frequented church in Auckland, with regularly around 1500 worshippers. It was a modern building:

> The building committee had planned a solid, elegant, and commodious house of worship, using ideas from British sources and blending these with others utilized in the Auckland Theatre Royal and the Opera House. An imposing exterior façade of Corinthian pillars led to a portico up a flight of six steps. The pediment supported by the pillars had molded capitals and pedestals. Lavish windows outlined by striated moldings and ornamented with pediments set off a high-pitched slated roof.[90]

It is difficult to assess the Booths' participation in the life of the church in detail. It can be assumed that they attended both Sunday services and Sunday School,[91] in which Mary Jane Booth was in charge of the Bible class for young women.

> Mention should also be made of the good services of Mesdames J. Blaikie, Battley, Booth, A.O. Knight, W. Lambourne and A. Thom, Misses M.A. Jones and S. Cooper, and Mr G. Anders, who have had charge of the Bible Classes for young women.[92]

It is also quite probable that Mary Jane Booth also participated in the Ladies' Benevolent Society (or, as it was called earlier, the Ladies' Sewing Society). The assessment of their participation is difficult, since the existing minute books deal mainly with the legal aspects of the life of the church, with admissions and dismissals being items of first importance, and it is at this level that a new growth step in Joseph Booth's life becomes visible, as on 28.9.1881 he was for the first time appointed to be a visitor to a candidate for baptism and church membership.

Such appointment as "visitor" to a baptismal candidate was a central part of Baptist polity at that time. For anyone who wanted to join the church, two visitors would be appointed by the monthly church (business) meeting. At the next meeting they would report the results of the visit to the church and (in most cases) propose the candidate for baptism and church membership. The church would then, by democratic vote of its members, decide about the application. When on 28.9.1881 the pastor submitted candidates for baptism and church membership, "Bros. Booth and Kelsey" were appointed for Mr and Mrs

---

[90] Craig Skinner, *Spurgeon and Son*, p. 89.
[91] For the history (and importance) see: *A Sunday School's Half-Century 1858-1908, Baptist Tabernacle, Auckland, New Zealand*, Auckland: 1908, 38 pp, richly illustrated. For details of the time of the Booths see p. 16. Mr S.G. Rountree was Superintendent.
[92] *A Sunday School's Half-Century 1858-1908*, p. 14.

Ritchie. On 19.10.1881 their (favourable) report was received by the church. Since then Joseph Booth was several times chosen to be a visitor.[93] This indicates that he was considered to be a well trusted member of the congregation. He never became a deacon in Auckland[94] as it happened later in Brighton Baptist Church in Melbournebut his position was most likely something like a prominent man in the second

level of church leadership. That he was appointed to such a task only about a year after arrival from England shows that the congregation quickly recognized his abilities.

In those years in Auckland all the visitors were male, so Mary Jane Booth could not be appointed as it later happened in Melbourne. That she belonged to the same second level of leadership as her husband

---

[93] In Nov. 1881 the minutes read: "Bro. Kelsey reported that Bro. Booth and himself had visited Mr. Kroll and had much pleasure in proposing that he be received into fellowship after baptism – carried."

[94] Even for a well respected and active member that would not have been easy, as the church was large, having 602 members in 1884 (Annual Report Wellesley Street Baptist Church, 1884).

is shown by the fact that she was in charge of the Sunday School class for the young women.

All this means that through membership in Auckland Baptist Church and through the change in the pastorate which they experienced, the Booths were influenced considerably by the Tabernacle spirituality. Later in his life Joseph Booth remembered two formative spiritual experiences which took place in Auckland. One of them is described thus:

> While worshipping in the Auckland Baptist Tabernacle [in 1885] he asked for a sign from God and opened his bible and read a prophecy: "I will send you to another land, there do the work that I shall command, and at the latter end will bring you again to this land."[95]

The second experience took place less than a year later, on 26.2.1886, his 35th birthday.

> His son presented him with a birthday card on which he had written what he considered his father's favourite text, a paraphrase of Proverbs 3:6 "Acknowledge Him in all thy ways, and he will direct thy path". Booth wrote later that he had assigned it as a punishment and had thought nothing of it: "But now, what was this? Was it the power of God confounding and convicting me, and repaying me for what I had said 20 years back to my father?" Booth was unable to eat, or go out but was "seized with such trembling & weeping that I was compelled to go back to my room overwhelmed & speechless, unable to pray but only to sob in a paroxysm of shame at the shallow and self-centred, superficial life I had led up to that day." Booth opened his bible to search for a sign, and found Isaiah 41:10 "Fear thou not, for I am with thee: be not dismayed, I am thy God: I will help thee: Yea, I will uphold thee." This led Booth to vow "Now if God will show I will try." Booth felt he had started a new life, "to find what God would 'show' He had for me to do".[96]

This experience, which can be classified as a deepening of spiritual life or as a rededication to personal discipleship, is quite in line with the Holiness Revival, though the description does not employ its technical

---

[95] Harry Langworthy, *"Africa for the African". The Life of Joseph Booth*, Blantyre: CLAIM-Kachere, 1996, p. 22, quoting *Sunday Times* (Johannesburg), 15. Aug. 1915. Reprinted as "Industrial Missions for Natives: Deportation of Founder", *Cape Times*, 16. Aug. 1915. – I could not identify the underlying Bible reference. The closest seems to me to be Genesis 28:15: "And behold, I am with thee, and will keep thee in all places whither thou goest, and will bring thee again into this land" (KJV).

[96] Harry Langworthy, *"Africa for the African". The Life of Joseph Booth*, p. 22, based on "Peace Calls".

language.[97] This experience of commitment was still general, not specific, but it implied an enhanced openness for God's leading in the future, and thus provided a base for things to work out in Melbourne.[98]

3. Move to Melbourne

For the Booth family, the years in Melbourne were to be good years. Mary Jane's health seems to have been steady, and in 1884 she had given birth to another child, a girl called Emily.[99] In business the Booths had done well and built a good house. They had done equally well in their spiritual life. They had joined a thriving congregation, had experienced its heydays under the ministry of a famous preacher, and had deepened their commitment to the service of Christ.

What made them move to Melbourne is not stated in the sources, but it is clear that they moved with the boom.[100] From 1880 onwards the economy of New Zealand stagnated or retrogressed,[101] but not in Auckland, where a boom, based on land (speculation) still continued at least till 1885.[102] While the boom in Auckland weakened, the boom in Melbourne, equally based on land (speculation), still blossomed, and many investors, who saw the signs of the times, moved to Melbourne taking lightly the truth that any boom must bust in due course. Only in

---

[97] The importance of the time in Auckland is also emphasized in Joseph Booth, "The Author's Apology", in Joseph Booth (Laura Perry [ed.]), *Africa for the African*, Blantyre: CLAIM-Kachere, ³1998(1897), p. 73-74.

[98] Since the specific expression of this general commitment was first formulated by Mary Jane Booth in Melbourne, in that she received for both of them the call to become missionaries, it can be assumed that she shared the earlier experience or made a similar commitment on her own.

[99] She seems to have been close to her father, and she came with him to Malawi in 1892 after her mother's death. About her experience there she wrote, much later in life, the manuscript "Into Africa with Father" (1939), which was published as Emily Booth-Langworthy, *This Africa was Mine*, Sterling Tract Enterprises, 1950. In her book she includes some information about Melbourne, probably from what she had heard from her father.

[100] Their house and plot was sold to Margaret Chapman of Auckland, a widow, on 11.2.1885 (Title Deed, vol. 15 Folio 281, 13 A 540).

[101] See R. Hawke, *The Making of New Zealand. An Economic History*, Cambridge University Press, 1985, p. 81; Greame Hunt, *The Rich List. Wealth and Enterprise in New Zealand 1820-2000*, Auckland: Reed, 2000, pp. 80-122 puts the time under the heading 'Crony Capitalism'.

[102] B. Easton, "Three New Zealand Depressions", in W.E. Willmot (ed.), *New Zealand and the World: Essays in Honour of Wolfgang Rosenberg*, Christchurch: University of Canterbury, 1980; R.J. Campbell, "'The Black Eighties' – Unemployment in New Zealand in the 1880s", *Australian Economic History Review*, xvi, pp. 67-82.

1886 a slowdown became obvious[103] and the first year with major unemployment. Booth was not involved in land speculation, but where there is a boom, his chances to sell milk (especially in more processed forms) would increase. As in Auckland, they joined the Baptist congregation closest to their residence, and they also found a church that was thriving and expanding, not a Tabernacle as in Auckland, but a regular Baptist Church, though, as the Tabernacle, influenced by the spirituality of the Holiness Revival.

Boom Years

Up to 1891 the Booths lived in an atmosphere of continuous boom. Economically they had been doing well in England. At 21, when they married, Joseph Booth was a commercial clerk in Rotherham, then in 1875 he became a dairyman in Sheffield. In 1879 the Booths emigrated to New Zealand. It is quite possible that Mary Jane's "weak lungs" were a major reason for their emigration, but the Booths also clearly did well economically.

When the Auckland boom showed the first signs of possibly being more like a bubble, Auckland investors began to transfer investments to Melbourne, where a similar boom was developing, equally based on land, and since it had started later, the bubble there burst later, too.

The Booths did well in Auckland, establishing a dairy business. That the business was successful is shown in the house they build at Auckland's north shore for £ 550.[104] Why they moved to Melbourne is not clear, but it is clear that they moved, consciously or not, with the boom.[105] Joseph Booth was not directly involved in it. There are no records that he participated in land speculation, the basis of both booms, or in related activities. But surely his dairy business in Auckland and later the "Milk Palace" in Melbourne would clearly prosper better in cities where there was much money going around, as was the case in both Auckland and Melbourne in his days. In both cases he had left when the inevitable economic downturn started.

---

[103] The church's regular income dropped by 200 pounds (Annual Report, 8/1882)

[104] Langworthy, *The Life of Joseph Booth*, p. 22.

[105] In the mid and late 1880s, "New Zealand investors began to send their money out of the country, mainly to Melbourne, where there was a building boom" and "thousands of men and women shifted to Australia in search of work" (Keith Sinclair [ed.], *The Oxford Illustrated History of New Zealand*, pp. 110-111).

Swanston Street and Town Hall Melbourne
(La Trobe Picture Collection, State Library of Victoria)

Booth had been successful in all his economic ventures in Britain, New Zealand and Australia. Why then did almost any other economic venture that he undertook as a missionary fail sooner or later?[106] Langworthy argues that spiritual arguments would override economic sense.[107] There is good evidence to support this interpretation. To this I would like to add the observation that, until he came to Africa, all his major economic calculations were made in boom situations, and many whose calculations proved correct under boom conditions had their calculations falsified when the bust came on.

The Booths had not only lived in a period of economic boom but also lived through a spiritual boom period. Auckland Tabernacle was a most successful church with a successful minister, the Baptist churches of

---

[106] Up to the coffee blight of 1929 both Zambezi Industrial Mission and Nyasa Industrial Mission were financially successful, though they did not generate the money for expansion which Booth had predicted (for ZIM see: *The Zambezi Mission. Missionaries Support Themselves for Thirty Years*, nd. [1930]). But that was without Booth. The initial period he worked with them was too short to assess economic success or failure.

[107] "Although Booth may have been ill-informed about facts and figures, or overly optimistic to the point of self-deception, he did not consciously mislead his public. Perhaps it would be accurate to contend that Booth was so sure of the rightness of the goals that if the facts and figures were not precise it did not matter much; the details could be worked out in the long run, as, after all, it was the will of God" (Harry Langworthy, *The Life of Joseph Booth*, p. 33).

Victoria went through a period of considerable expansion, and within that picture Brighton was a leading light.[108] This may explain, to some extent, the spiritual optimism in many of Booth's calculations.

The owners of the Milk Palace

Harry Langworthy writes that Booth was "a partner in a thriving chain of restaurants".[109] I found the partner, but not the chain. In the *Melbourne Directory* of Sands and McDougall of 1887 till 1890, George Anthony Brown[110] and Joseph Booth are listed as the proprietors of the Melbourne Milk Palace Co., 111 Swanston Street, just opposite Melbourne Town Hall, not far from Collins Street, the "best" of Melbourne's city streets.

In a boom period a milk palace[111] in such a situation should be an economic success.[112] Booth's (or Brown's?) innovative spirit is shown by the fact that they are credited for having introduced artificial (electric) refrigeration in Melbourne.[113] At the same time the first attempts were made at electrical street lightening, while the Melbourne trams (which today make Melbourne famous) had still to wait years for electricity.[114]

---

[108] In the Victorian Baptist (1891, p. 112) Brighton Baptist Church reports: "God is greatly blessing us just now in our work, especially in the Sunday school. A spirit of deep and earnest inquiry is abroad, and many of the young souls have already come to a decision for the Lord."

[109] Harry Langworthy, *The Life of Joseph Booth*, p. 23.

[110] Resident Carpenter Street, Brighton.

[111] Today the milk palace might go by the name of ice cream parlour, and the shops opposite town hall today allow one more to imagine a parlour than a palace. It seems that the name was consciously chosen in opposition to the "gin palaces" frequent in the city. I imagine that many of them also would have been more parlours (or dens?) than palaces.

[112] In the block opposite Town Hall there are still about 8 restaurants and eating places, including a strawberry parlour (1996).

[113] Harry Langworthy, *The Life of Joseph Booth*, p. 23, based on "Peace Calls", "Into Africa" p. 66, Emily Langworthy - Shepperson, 21 April 1954.

[114] Melbourne today has over 40 tram lines, one of them the City Circle. Melbourne is the only city with a restaurant in a tram travelling through the city.

When the Booths came to Melbourne, the city had about 900,000 inhabitants.[115] All of Victoria had more than a million inhabitants.[116] The population was growing, and a big land boom, in which speculators bought chunks of land (mostly on credit) to resell with high profit in smaller plots, had brought large amounts of money into Melbourne, much of it being investments from Britain.

Collins Street, Melbourne

Only a small part of that land boom was based on sound economics. In 1889 the land boom started to run into problems,[117] and in 1890 it burst. The speculators got stuck with chunks of land whose loans they could no longer service. Many light-hearted attitudes and many fraudulent business practices came to light and many an honest small investor lost much or all.[118]

---

[115] For 1881 the figure of 862,000 is given. It was by then the largest city in Australia and the seventh largest city in the whole of the British Empire (Ray Dahlitz, *Secular Who's Who. A Bibliographical Directory of Freethinkers, Secularists, Rationalists, Humanists, and others involved in Australia's Secular Movement from 1850 onwards*, Melbourne: nd., p. 3).

[116] Government estimated the population of Victoria to have been 1,075,569 on 30.9.1887 ("Notable Events", 14.12.1888).

[117] "New insolvent: J. Alcock, freeholder, South Yarra, caused by fall in value of real estate" ("Notable Events", 16.2.1989).

[118] The Baptist denominational journal had already commented in 1889: "The Land Boom appears to have collapsed – we hope finally, for it was a social epidemic, well named a "fever", and as disastrous to healthful commercial life as its name suggests. We must sincerely commiserate the many whose worst experience is not disappointment in the large prospective gains. Alas! Some are losing the accumulations of many years of honest toil, in

The bust of the land boom was indeed the beginning of the following deep depression,[119] but to most contemporaries that became only obvious in 1892, *after* Booth had already sold his business. The year of 1890 was still a year of economic success, and the banking and finance companies in Melbourne still flourished.[120] Equally a sign for Melbourne's economic vitality was its strong labour movement, and it was in Melbourne that the idea of the eight hours working day was born.[121]

Another sign of economic boom was the rapid expansion of the railway system. The Booths found the Brighton Railway already in existence,[122] and while they lived there, a horse drawn tram line was built from East Brighton to Central Brighton.[123] Much of the railway

---

legitimate paths of industry. Revelations are made of shameful sacrifices of principle in the unhallowed greed for gold, which makes us blush for the Christian name. Poverty, with honour, were infinitely preferable to the disclosures which are now being made, by force of circumstances. With many, let us hope with most, their only blame was that attaching to a simplicity which allowed itself to be gulled in the hope of sharing sudden gain, wholly disproportionate to their investments. God, who makes our backslidings correct us, will, we are sure, yet work some high and lasting good out of our calamities. O the 'uncertainty of riches'. O the unchanging love and care of God" (*The Victorian Freeman*, Feb 1889, p. 22).

[119] The wider effects of the bust of the land boom were felt in the international loan market: On 6.2.1889 the "Notable Events" report that of the South Australian loan of £ 1,317,800 at 3,5%, only £ 553,700 were subscribed at or above minimum.

[120] In the *Melbourne Directory Sands and McDougall* 1890, bank and finance company adverts occupied the first 30 of 68 pages. By 1890 only one housing bank (General and Mutual Investment and Building Society) had obviously got itself into trouble, because John Bellin, the managing director, embezzled the funds ("Notable Events", 1.9.1890). But there is a crook everywhere, isn't there?

[121] Its birth was in 1865. 4,000 participated in the 33rd anniversary celebration. 80,000 marched a year later in a "brilliant demonstration of the various trade societies" ("Notable Events", *The Age Annual, 1882-1890*).

[122] Today part of the Metro suburban electrical train system.

[123] In 1890 a daughter church of Brighton Baptist was opened in Brighton East (*The Victorian Freeman*, Nov. 1890).

expansion was credit financed, the dangers of which became obvious only later, while in Booth's time this expansion added to the boom.

City Circle Line, Melbourne

Old type trams in the Museum (Melbourne)

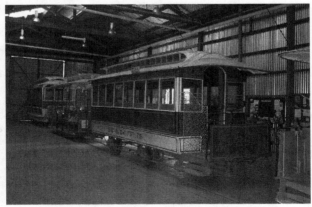

*Today
Melbourne is
worldwide
the city with
the largest
tramway
network*

During his years in Melbourne (1887-1891), until he sold his property,[124] everything was economically all right for Booth. He had not speculated in land but invested in sound business, so he came out unscathed and I can imagine that he went to Central Africa with the conviction that his business calculations had been sound and that in future enterprises he could be equally successful.

4. Brighton Baptist Church

On 28 September 1887 Mary Jane and Joseph Booth applied for membership of Brighton Baptist Church, which was granted to them on arrival of their transfer letters from Auckland Tabernacle.[125]

The reason for joining Brighton Baptist Church and not any other Baptist Church was most probably their residence in Male Street, a quiet residential street which connects the south of North Brighton to Middle Brighton, running south of the railway line, and in easy walking distance to Brighton Baptist Church off Bay Street in North Brighton. It

---

[124] In Booth's bible there is an entry against Matthew 28,19-20, dated 24 January 1891, relating to the sale (Langworthy, *The Life of Joseph Booth*, p. 23). This may well have been the date of the decision (or the challenge and the decision), since the sale took place 1 May 1891 (Booth, "The Author's Apology", p. 75).
[125] Brighton Baptist Church Minutes Book, 28.9.1887.

is worth to note that they did not join the Church of Christ on Male Street, which would have been even closer and which had a theology related to that of the Baptists and which Joseph Booth later introduced into Malawi.[126]

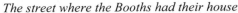

The street where the Booths had their house

---

[126] Booth introduced the Church of Christ into Malawi in 1907 through Hills and Hollis and Ellerton Kundago, a Yao converted in Bulawayo Church of Christ (Langworthy, *The Life of Joseph Booth*, pp. 199-201; Ernest Gray, *The Early History of the Churches of Christ Missionary Work in Nyasaland, Central Africa, 1907-1930*, Cambridge, 1981; C.B. Shelburne, *History of the Church of Christ in Malawi*, np., nd., 4 pp. provides a brief, factual account of the history of the Church of Christ in southern Malawi. (Copy at the Baptist Theological Seminary, Lilongwe). The Churches of Christ centred on Dowa also go back to Booth, but indirectly. He started the work as the Baptist Industrial Mission of Scotland in 1895 (Langworthy, *The Life of Joseph Booth*, pp. 70-73) and in 1929 it was transferred to the Church of Christ (Rendell Day, *From Gowa Industrial Mission to Landmark Missionary Baptists: One Hundred Years of Baptist Churches in Malawi, 1894-1994*, Zomba: Kachere, 2008 (Kachere Documents no. 52). A full history of the various branches of the Churches of Christ in Malawi is being written by Mark Thiesen as a PhD for Mzuzu University.

Map of Brighton Today

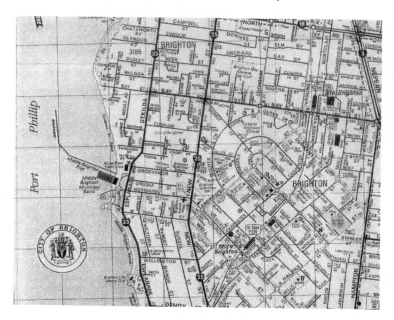

Church of Christ on Male Street, Brighton, where the Booths lived

Brighton Baptist Church 1996

The Brighton congregation had been started in 1851 as a daughter church of Collins Street, the mother of all Baptist Churches in Victoria.[127] Decline started in 1859, the church was closed 15.8.1864, with 21 members transferring back to Collins Street. 17 members reopened the church 30.6.1867, and this was the beginning of a steady development. When the Booths joined, the church had 90 members,[128] a church building of its own and a settled pastor, Rev S. Howard.[129] During Howard's pastorate (1886-1894) Brighton Baptist Church was without major problems, it was socially cohesive and spiritually alive.[130]

---

[127] *Links with the Past. The Centenary of Brighton Baptist Church 1851-1951*, Melbourne: 1951. Founded 12.3.1851, a wood church was built in 1853 for £ 546.

[128] Brighton Annual Report to Assembly, 30.10.1887. The preceding year brought: 11 new members, 2 transferred, 1 death. - This was a good growth for any congregation. Baptist count only baptized members, and baptism is on confession of faith. Young children are an important part of the congregation, as their strong emphasis on Sunday School and youth groups shows, but they are not counted as [full] members. - In the preceding year the Sunday School had grown from an average 80 to 85 in attendance (ibid.). By 1889 the congregation had 120 members (Annual Report, Brighton Baptist Church, 1889).

[129] Stephen Howard was first pastor of Jamestown and Gawler in South Australia, then of Brighton, after that of Kew in Victoria, Perth in Tasmania and briefly in Adelaide. He retired to Kew and died 13.8.1939, aged 97 years. 1888/89 he was President of the Baptist Union of Victoria (*The Victorian Baptist Witness*, 5.9.1939).

[130] "The church greatly prospered" (F.J. Wilkin, *Baptists in Victoria. Our First Century 1838-1938*, Melbourne 1939, p. 37).

The church and its pastor had a strong evangelistic interest,[131] members were willing to invest love and labour into the development of their church.[132] The congregation put much emphasis on Sunday School work, and when the Christian Endeavour idea spread to Victoria, Brighton was one of the many congregations which took it up enthusiastically.[133]

While the Booths were members, the church building was extended and renovated, to be more comfortable and to increase the Sunday School facilities.[134] There was

> Progress all along the line ... well attended and earnest week night services, often filling our room to overflowing with devout and praying worshippers ... Several new devotional gatherings have been inaugurated and are maintained with earnestness, specially by the ladies of the Church and congregation.[135]

Such a happy development of a Baptist congregation was not infrequent in those days. The Victoria Baptist Association as a whole was growing, a trend which only stopped around 1900.[136] Altogether the Booths came from a thriving Baptist context in New Zealand to a thriving Baptist context in Victoria. This seems to me to be another base for Booth's (at times unrealistic) optimism in Africa.

---

[131] "The pastor was an evangelical preacher. His messages were full of fire and challenge, and no effort was spared to bring people to the church" (*Links with the Past, The Centenary of Brighton Baptist Church 1851-1951*, Melbourne: 1951 p. 6).

[132] Report in *The Victorian Freeman*, 4.11.1888.

[133] Report in *The Victorian Freeman* for 1891. Christian Endeavour was an innovative youth movement founded 1881 in the USA with its roots in the Holiness Revival. It offered many new leadership opportunities for Christian women.

[134] "During the year considerable outlay has been incurred in the renovation of our historic time worn Church structure; the comfort of which is greatly increased by the erection of a Vestibule and complete interior refitting, and also by the enlargement of the old school room for Sunday School work. Some considerable portion of the cost of these enlargements has been met by an advance of £ 500 (Brighton Church Report to Assembly, October 1890).

[135] *The Victorian Freeman*, 4.11.1888.

[136] From 1894 onwards money had already become somewhat scarce due to the economic depression. By then Booth was already in Malawi, but the scarcity of money affected the support the Victoria Baptists were likely to give to Booth.

Drawing of the improvement of the South Brighton Baptist Church

Joseph Booth, deacon and evangelist

The Booth family must have joined wholeheartedly in the life and work of their new congregation, for when in January 1888 for the first time deacons were elected,[137] Joseph Booth was one of the five deacons.[138] Mary Jane Booth, being a woman, was not considered eligible as a deacon in those days. The church records show that Joseph Booth began immediately to do his share in the work. One of the major formal duties of deacons was "to wait upon" [visit] prospective members and

---

[137] Up to that time the elected office bearers had acted informally as deacons. In the Baptist pattern which Brighton followed the pastor is the only elder, assisted by deacons. Other Baptist churches have multiple church elders, and the minister is one of them.

[138] The deacons were Rees, Derbyshire, Chambers, Booth and Brewer. In February Knight was added to the number of deacons (Brighton Church Minutes Book 4.1.1888 and 29.2.1888).

to recommend them for baptism and (after that) for membership.[139]

Very close to Joseph Booth's heart was the evangelistic endeavour of the church, "missionary work" as Baptists call it. His first effort was to start a Young Men's Mutual Improvement Association together with Mr Darbyshire.[141] This could be interpreted, using more modern terminology, as "social involvement", but for Booth that was never separate from evangelism, just as in all the Tabernacle Baptist churches.[142] Booth then carried his evangelistic ministry further afield. He formed a little band for street evangelism,[143] and in order to be free enough for that he even resigned his position as a deacon in July 1889,[144] much to the regret of the congregation.[145]

The street preaching took place outside the geographical area of Brighton at Queen's Wharf close to the main railway station at Flinders Street.[146] At Queen's Wharf there were plenty of people, and there he met with the "evangelistic" activities of the Secularists, led by Joseph

---

[139] The minutes concentrate on formal activities, but these visits were only given to members who also contributed in informal ways to the life of the congregation.

[140] Baptist Theology does not distinguish between missions at home and abroad. Since William Carey (1792) mission was always mission in 5 (or 6) continents. Heathen could equally be found in Britain as in the islands of Oonalashka (William Carey, *An Enquiry into the Obligations of Christians to Use Means for the Conversion of the Heathens. In which the religious state of the different nations of the world, the success of former undertakings and the practicability of further undertakings, are considered*, Leicester 1792, pp. 13 and 52).

[141] Brighton Church Minutes Book 29.2.1888.

[142] He probably copied the idea from Auckland, where in 1884 the Young Men's Mutual Improvement Association "is in full activity, and receives a hearty support from our young men, many of whom are among the best workers in our Sunday Schools and Church agencies" (Annual Report Wellesley Street Baptist Church 1884).

[143] "Some three or four of our brethren, led by Mr. J. Booth, are earnestly engaged in evangelistic street preaching, both in Brighton itself, and in other localities as the way opens, and not without tokens of the Master's approval in the awakening of spiritual interest in the irreligious" (*The Victorian Freeman*, March 1889, p. 42, report from Brighton Baptist Church).

[144] "The question of Mr. Booth was discussed, and letters were read from him stating his reasons for resigning. Moved by Mr. Chambers, seconded by Mr. Derbyshire, that the resignation be received with regret and that Divine blessings may rest on his city labours. Moved by Mr. Howard, seconded by Mr. Rees, that the Church recognise their sense [?] of obligation they are under (Brighton Church MinuteS Book, 17.7.1889).

[145] *The Victorian Freeman*, August 1889, p. 119. - This decision did not mean a withdrawal from the activities of the congregation. The minutes show that he was active in the church meetings and continued to be entrusted with visiting applicants for membership.

[146] "Mixed News," *The Baptist Freeman*, October 1889, p. 138.

Symes.[147] This led Booth to attend the evening "services" of the Secularists, where usually Symes was the lecturer (40 minutes) and critical responses were invited (10 minutes).[148]

During those encounters early 1891 or late 1890 Symes challenged Booth not to throw his pearls to the pigs in Melbourne where nobody wanted them but to offer them to the savages in Central Africa.

> Of course you have heard, or read his final orders, "go ye out, to the uttermost parts of the earth - Lo I am with you." Are there no savages in Central Africa and if so, why do you not go to them instead of casting these doubtful pearls where no one wants them? Why don't you go without purse, without weapons, without societies; is not "Lo, I am with you" good enough? Have you forgotten this Christ's message to men of possessions, "Sell all thou hast and give to the poor?" When is the sale coming off? When shall you start to be a Christian?[149]

This Booth then did, selling his profitable business on 1 May 1891,[150] though he was convinced that the people of that area were no savages at all.[151]

Mary Jane Booth

Even in those early years women were important in Baptist congregations, though few official positions of leadership were open to them. During the Booths' time in Brighton a woman deacon was yet unthinkable, but some change in women's position took place. In 1888 the church minutes mention women only as applicants for baptism, but from December 1889 they also name women as visitors to female applicants for baptism, a task that up to then had been carried out by (male) deacons. There would always be two visitors, and Mrs Booth was part of the first pair[152] and then was frequently asked to perform

---

147 "Mr. T.T. Phillips will lecture on the Queen's Wharf tomorrow (Sunday) afternoon, at 3 o'clock. Subject:- 'Has Man a Soul?' The Lecture will be illustrated by means of diagrams. John Love, Sec. A.S.A" (*The Liberator, 1*889, p. 533).

148 *The Liberator*, 21.2.1891, p. 2297.

149 Harry Langworthy, *The Life of Joseph Booth*, p. 23, quoting from "Peace Calls"; corroborated in "Into Africa", 43-44. Bible: 24 January 1891, Matt. 28:19-20.

150 Joseph Booth, "The Author's Apology", p. 75. - In the *Melbourne Directory Sands and McDougall* of 1891 the entry reads: "Swanston Street 111 Andrew G., Milk Palace".

151 He was convinced that "One is your Master, even Christ, and all ye are brethren." (Principle k of his proposal for a mission in Central Africa in: Joseph Booth, "The Greatest Work of the World - A Plea for Missionary Enterprise", *Missionary Review of the World* 1892, pp. 573-580), cf. Langworthy, *The Life of Joseph Booth*, p. 27.

152 The other visitor was Mrs Arwood, if I read the entry correctly (Brighton Church Minutes Book 11.12.1889).

the same task.[153] The fact that she was called upon so often for this service shows that she was one of the five or so leading married women in Brighton church. Though there is no written record available to me on that, I assume that she was also a leading participant in the Ladies' Serving Society, which was in those years the major activity of women in the church.[154] Women also had a share in teaching children and youth and also in music,[155] but though it is quite a possibility, I found no evidence that Mary Jane Booth participated in either.

As so often in the records, the women's voice is muted, but here at least it is strong enough to ascertain that she was a leading member of the church and that the claim that she shared her husband's missionary vision is well grounded. She was not reluctant to sell all and go, and only death from pneumonia on October 9, 1891 prevented her from going. It may even be that she was the first to express the call. One night she dreamed that a messenger stood at the foot of the bed and said, "Come to China", and after discussion with her husband they decided to sell what they had and to become missionaries.[156]

That she dreamt of China is not surprising. As a "regular" Victorian Baptist she should have dreamt of a messenger from India, since that was the long established and much loved mission field of the Victorian Baptists, but being a Baptist of the Tabernacle variety, the type of mission she would relate to were the faith missions, innovative and interdenominational,[157] of which the China Inland Mission was the most famous and possibly the only one of them then in reach in Victoria.[158] At the end of May 1891 Joseph Booth travelled to London to find a

---

[153] This was not infrequently because the church was growing at that time.

[154] It is quite probable, based on evidence elsewhere, that the ladies' meetings, beyond producing items for sale in favour of the renovation of the church and preparing teas and coffees, had a major spiritual and social component. It is hardly imaginable that Mrs Booth did not take part.

[155] In 1889 Miss Alexander was the church's organist, her predecessor was male.

[156] Harry Langworthy, *The Life of Joseph Booth*, p. 24, based on "Into Africa", pp. 43-44.

[157] For the innovative aspects of the faith missions see: Klaus Fiedler, *The Story of the Faith Missions*, pp. 33. Major innovative aspects were that women were considered to be missionaries in their own rights, that ordination was not necessary, that evangelism was urgent and had priority, and that missionary work should not be restricted to the well educated.

[158] From 1890 – 1964, 513 missionaries from Australia and New Zealand joined the China Inland Mission. The second to join was Charles H. Parsons from Victoria, no. 20 was Marie Box (joined March 1891, retired 1895). Altogether 161 missionaries from Victoria joined (Marcus L. Loane, *The Story of the CIM in Australia 1890-1964*, Auckland: CIM/OMF, 1965, pp. 151-168.

mission to join, and he did approach the China Inland Mission, but was considered to be too old.[159]

Joseph Booth and his family, c.1890

Edward and Emily Booth

When the Booths joined Brighton Baptist Church, their son Edward was eleven and their daughter Emily three years of age.[160] It can be assumed that they attended church with their parents as well as the Sunday School, which at that time was in a strong upward development.

On 18 December 1889 Edward applied for baptism, and since his visitors (Messrs. Derbyshire and Coles) reported favourably, he was accepted for baptism and church membership.[161] One and a half year

[159] This was not the only mission he approached that rejected him (the age limit for candidates in those days tended to be 30 years). See Langworthy, *The Life of Joseph Booth*, p. 24. It is quite probable that the Booths did not understand the dream as a call exclusively to China but as a general call to missionary work.

[160] Edward was born in Sheffield in 1876, Emily was born on 4 August 1884 in Auckland.

[161] Mr Chambers proposed and Mr Brewer seconded that he be received into church fellowship after baptism (Brighton Church Minutes Book 18.12.1889).

later his sister Emily applied, too, and was accepted on the grounds of an equally positive report.[162] Edward's baptism at 13 years of age is well in line with Baptist practice, but with Emily the early age of seven is surprising.[163] Edward felt the missionary call, probably in 1890, when he started to head his letters "Africa for Christ".[164] Edward died aged 19 as a missionary in Mitsidi from malaria and exhaustion due to a trip down the Zambezi with John Chilembwe to bring in supplies for the mission.[165] Emily did not follow up her childhood commitment to become a missionary.[166]

5. The political and social challenge

Around 1890 the colony of Victoria was politically full of confidence.[167] The colony had more than one million people, a good amount of self-government and was moving towards a leading role in the coming federation of Australia.[168]

In political and social life, there was still a strong Christian influence. One could even be fined for selling a quart of milk on a Sunday, though houses of ill repute usually seem to have been able to escape police attention. Victoria was very strong in organized labour. Trade unions flourished,[169] and Melbourne has the honour of being the birthplace of

---

[162] Brighton Church Minutes Book 22.4.1891 and 29.5.1891.

[163] Baptists baptize on confession of faith, and though they do not doubt children's faith, in most cases baptism is only possible after reaching the "age of discretion", maybe at 12 or 10, when a decision of faith, which should last for life, can be made.

[164] Joseph Booth, *Africa for the African*, ed. by Laura Perry, 1998 [1897], p. 105 (opposite p. 16 in ^{2}1897 edition).

[165] Ibid., with a picture of the graveyard.

[166] She also left the keeping of the Sabbath together with her husband Harry Langworthy. Booth was deeply disappointed and tried to use parental authority to make her change (Joseph Booth - Emily Langworthy 13.11.1909). Emily Langworthy is the grandmother of Harry Langworthy, the author of Booth's biography.

[167] Joseph Symes called the whole thing not a success but a muddle.

[168] Achieved on 1 January 1901, with Victoria's leading role being strongly contested by New South Wales, so that the issue of the capital was later decided in favour of Canberra, in New South Wales, but not Sydney, about half way between Sidney and Melbourne.

[169] A major expression of trade unionism was the big Trades Hall in LaTrobe Street, with its own council and many activities, like the "Working Men's College, giving instructions ... at low rates of fee" (*Melbourne Directory Sands and McDougall* 1891).

the "Eight-Hour Day Movement"[170]. On 21.4.1890, 80,000 trade union-ists marched to celebrate the 34th anniversary.[171] In 1888, the Tramway

'All the World Over' – The Worker cartoonist in 1903 still saw the strike as labour's main weapon

Employees Union declared a strike to establish the closed shop system,[172] and in 1890, there was a major strike in the harbour.[173]

Trade was in those days an essential part of politics, and in the constant struggle between free traders and protectionists the latters' voice was increasingly heard.[174] The trade unions, who for their part aspired to the closed shop system, demanded for the industries protection against imports.[175]

Related to ideas of protectionism were anti-Chinese sentiments which led to an ugly campaign against Chinese immigration, with a major anti-Chinese meeting taking place in the Town Hall, presided

---

[170] It's birth was 1856. 4000 participated in the 33rd anniversary celebration. ("Notable Events", *The Age Annual*, 1874-1876, 1879-1880, 1882-1890").

[171] "The 34th anniversary of Eight-Hours' Day celebrated by a brilliant demonstration of the various trade societies, of whom 80,000 members marched in the procession" ("Notable Events", 21.4.1890).

[172] This attempt failed. The decision was made on 12.2.1888, the strike collapsed on 17.2.1888. There were seven completed tramway lines at that time ("Notable Events").

[173] It started 20.8.90 and was still deadlocked on 23.9.98 ("Notable Events").

[174] "Duty on imported barley and oats from 2s to 3s per cent ("Notable Events" 11.9.1888).

[175] "The Trades' Hall Council protested against orders being sent to Scotland by the Melbourne Harbour Trust for two dredges while they could be made in Melbourne" ("Notable Events" 24.1.1889).

over by no one else than the mayor of Melbourne,[176] demanding what later became known as the "white Australia policy".[177]

The intellectual climate was not fully free, but for the times quite liberal. There was almost equal freedom for Christianity and Secularism,[178] there was freedom of speech, and the University (founded 1853)[179] was flourishing, with the number of women students growing.[180] In terms of women's professional development, Victoria was ahead, with the first Australian woman medical doctor being accredited in 1890.[181] Women had no right yet to vote, but would receive it for the Australian Parliament in 1902.[182]

Though the direct evidence is scanty, I think that some educated guesses can be made as to Booth's attitude to those issues and that some deductions can be made as to their influence on Booth's life as a missionary.

In general, the Tabernacle Baptists had a strong feeling of social concern, not just limited to the need for charity. Charles Haddon Spurgeon was very much involved, not only with his big orphanage, but also in providing elementary English education. The social activities may have been even more extended in A.G. Brown's West London

---

[176] "Notable Events" 1.5.1888.

[177] This was given legal form by the Immigration Restrictions Act 1901, designed "to exclude cheap Asian labour and to avert racial conflict", not to be repealed until 1973 (*Compton's Interactive Encyclopedia*, Cambridge, MA: The Learning Company, 1998).

[178] The school system was moving towards increasing state control. Religion could be taught in school, but Secularists complained that they were not allowed to teach their religion in schools (but if allowed there would have been very few Secularists to get all the teaching done...).

[179] This was the second Australian university, after Sydney, founded 1850.

[180] "Annual commencement of Melbourne University celebrated in Wilson Hall. Nearly 50 ladies attended in cap and gown, two of whom took the degree of BA and one of MA" ("Notable Events", 7.4.1888). On 30.3.1889 seven of 60 degrees were awarded to women.

[181] "Miss E. Constance Stone, the first Australian lady doctor, granted registration of her diploma by the Medical Board of Victoria" ("Notable Events", 7.2.1890). *The Melbourne Directory Sands and McDougall* 1890 records: "16 Collins St, Miss Emma C. Stone, physician".

[182] The first country worldwide to give women the vote was New Zealand in 1893, the Commonwealth of Australia granted the suffrage in 1902, and only in 1906 became Finland the first European country to allow full women's suffrage. Victoria granted the right to vote in 1908.

Tabernacle.[183] The Mission Hall of Thomas Barnardo,[184] of which the Guinness family of faith mission fame were members, is another important example because the Guinness family and their East London Training Institute (ELTI) were Booth's main missionary contact in London.

Lucy Guinness once disguised herself and worked and lived for six weeks as a factory worker.[185]

The official magazine of the Victoria Baptists several times took a strong stand against the anti-Chinese agitation.[186] Booth must have read this paper,[187] and the opinion expressed tallies with his conviction that under Christ all were one.

In his evangelistic work, he was in constant dialogue with the Secularists and though they and their leader Symes were not in good books with the organized Trade Union movement, the Secularists were very eager to point out social injustices. Booth was an employer and never expressed clear Socialist thinking, but his complaints against the generous lifestyle of whites in Malawi[188] and his willingness to pay

---

[183] A.G. Brown was perhaps the leading personality among the students at Spurgeon's Theological Seminary, which he had founded for those who were called by God to the ministry but had not had the opportunity to attend the necessary schools for "regular" theological training. Brown's Tabernacle, though clearly Baptist, only (and strongly) supported the interdenominational faith missions, not the Baptist Mission (George E. Page, *A.G.B., The Story of the Life and Work of Archibald Geikie Brown*, London 1944). - Brown was invited to become pastor of Melbourne Albert Street Baptist Church, but declined (*The Victorian Baptist*, 1890, pp. 83 and 115).

[184] After a meeting with Hudson Taylor, Thomas Barnardo decided to join the nascent China Inland Mission. Hudson Taylor accepted him and told him that he should get his medical degree first (A.J. Broomhall, *Survivors' Pact*, London: Hodder and Stoughton and Overseas Missionary Fellowship, 1984). While he was studying in London, he saw the plight of the many orphans and started to work among them. That was as far as he got on his way to China, but he remained a missionary all his life (David Fessenden, *Father to Nobody's Children: The Life of Thomas J. Barnardo*, Halesowen: Christian Literature Crusade, 1995.

[185] After that she wrote a booklet about her experience and the (dismal) conditions she had found: Lucy Guinness, *Only a Factory Girl*, London, 1886.

[186] "The Anti-Chinese agitation is assuming a very Anti-Christian form. In their eagerness to crush the alien race, some persons who should know better, are forgetting their natural kinship with them, and the claims which the common redemption imposes (*The Victorian Freeman*, Jan. 1888, p. 20).

[187] Compared to the number of Baptists in Victoria its circulation was high, and it can hardly be imagined that a leading Baptist would not read it.

[188] In 1892 Booth wrote this to Caldwell: Candidly now, is it not a marvelous picture to see elegantly robed men, at some hundreds of pounds yearly cost, preaching a gospel of self-denial to men and women slaves, with only a very scrap of goat skin about their loins, compelled to work hard from daylight to dark six, but more often seven days a week, for

higher wages when establishing industrial missions there can not be explained by the labour situation in Victoria, but it can be seen as a supporting motive to his Christian concern that justice be done to all, even African labourers.

I am not aware of any comments of Booth on the theme of female advancement, and the fact that his wife died of pneumonia[189] before she became a missionary deprives us of decided evidence of his attitude. Booth shared with all the faith missions the then innovative idea that women, whether married or not, were missionaries in their own right, and just before the Booths decided to go to Africa, Marie Box, a single woman of his congregation, had joined the China Inland Mission,[190] sharing her farewell meeting with four other lady missionaries.[191]

In Booth's later carrier, single women missionaries play hardly any role nor do married women seem to have played much of a separate role. Booth's second wife Annie, from the Isle of Wight, whom he married on 4 March 1896, was aware of her own call as a missionary[192] and obviously shared in her husband's efforts and made her own contribution.[193] Booth was not a campaigner for women's rights, but sharing the most progressive position within his religious context, he did definitely

---

calico costing five pence per week the men and two pence halfpenny the women, and this calico not theirs but their owners? I have never felt so ashamed of myself and my fellow countrymen as I have since coming here. Either we ought to stop spreading the Gospel or conform to its teaching amidst such a needy cloud of witnesses as Central Africa presents."

[189] Maybe there is a connection between the "weak lungs" that contributed to her emigration to New Zealand and her early death.

[190] This did not destroy the congregation's involvement with the missionary work of the Baptist Missionary Society. "On 5th August our dear friend, Miss Emily Chambers, who has lately consecrated her young life to mission work, gave the first of her farewell missionary addresses .... Mr. Melville, on the same evening, gave an interesting account as to how he also decided to become a missionary" (Brighton Report in *The Victorian Baptist*, September 1891, p. 172).

[191] "We held a meeting to take farewell of CIM missionaries Misses Box, Chapman, Gold, Fleming and Henry on 6th February - Miss Box being a member with us. Our pastor presided. The church was crowded" (Report from Brighton in *The Victorian Baptist* April 1891, p. 71).

[192] She had prayed at Livingstone's grave that God would some day find a way for her to serve in Africa (Langworthy, *The Life of Joseph Booth*, p. 73-74).

[193] Charles Domingo, founder of the Seventh Day Baptist churches in Malawi, regularly corresponded with Annie Booth (Charles Domingo, *Letters of Charles Domingo*, ed. Harry Langworthy, Zomba: University of Malawi, Sources for the Study of Religion in Malawi no. 9, 1983).

nothing to slow down their progress.[194] He must have read and most probably shared the views expressed in the obituary for Catherine Booth, one of the founders of the Salvation Army:

> Mrs. [Catherine] Booth is dead. Perhaps no woman of the century is more sincerely or worthily mourned. She was the very heart of the great movement, which has thrust its roots into every English-speaking community. Her ability and sanctity have been the strongest forces in securing respectful attention to the teachings of the Army. Her children, natural and spiritual, rise up and call her blessed.[195]

6. The intellectual challenge

While the labour movement produced the social challenge for Booth, the atheist Secularist Movement produced the intellectual challenge. Possibly the first contact was established during Booth evangelistic efforts at Queen's Wharf in Melbourne, but the challenge was not only missionary but intellectual, too, because in his youth he had been an Atheist himself, and his drift back to Christianity had started when he read a book by the agnostic Thomas Paine, who wrote that there was no doubt that a person called Jesus really existed.[196]

Booth's exchanges with the Secularists were of major importance, one of them constituting what he later termed "the Atheist's call" and which pushed him further to start his missionary career. During one of the Sunday evening "debates", Joseph Symes challenged him:

> Are there no savages in Central Africa and if so, why do you not go to them instead of casting these doubtful pearls where no one wants them? Why don't you go without purse, without weapons, without societies?[197]

Langworthy's assessment of the context of this exchange is based on Emily Booth's recollection, in which Booth was an equal partner in a series of public discussions in front of large audiences. Melbourne data do not support this arrangement, but they do support the evaluation of the events for Booth's career.

---

[194] He was slow in transferring the women liberationist aspects of his evangelical conviction to African women, an attitude shared by many faith missionaries.

[195] *The Victorian Baptist*, November 1890, p. 163. The scriptural allusion is to the independent and admirable woman in the book of Proverbs. After all that she has done for her husband, her children, the poor and afflicted, in trade, industry and management, "Her children arise and call her blessed" (Proverbs 31:28). One of Mrs Booth's books was: Catherine Booth, *Female Ministry. Woman's Right to Preach the Gospel*, London: Morgan & Chase, nd.

[196] Harry Langworthy, *The Life of Joseph Booth*, p. 20.

[197] Harry Langworthy, *The Life of Joseph Booth*, p. 23.

The Secularist Movement in Australia

In the last quarter of the 19th century the English-speaking world was still very much Christian or at least pretended to be so. Still there was also conscious infidelity, related to the ideas of the Enlightenment[198] with strong influences from France, in various forms: atheism,[199] deism,[200] secularism[201] and, with different sources, theosophy.[202] For Melbourne the great figure of the British secularist movement was Charles Bradlaugh,[203] whose writings were advertised every week in the *Liberator.*[204]

His death in 1891 was mourned with great prominence in the *Liberator*. Thomas Paine was also claimed by the Melbourne Secularists as one of their "fathers", in spite of the fact that he had retained a vague belief in the possibility of a God.[205] They regularly celebrated his birthday, made more attractive by the fact that his birthday was the same as that of Symes (29.1.1737/1841).

---

[198] 17th and 18th centuries. "Its goal was to understand the world and man's place in it solely on the basis of reason without turning to religious beliefs" (*Compton's Interactive Encyclopedia*).

[199] The belief that there is no God.

[200] "Deism advocates natural religion based on reason rather than revelation, believes that God is apart from human affairs" (*Compton's Interactive Encyclopedia*).

[201] "A system of philosophy which accepts demonstrated truth only for its standard, and reason for its guide" (E. Skinner, *The Secularists' Guide. A Book for Young and Old*, Sydney, nd. [1890?], p. 11.)

[202] In 1875 the Russian Helena Petrovna Blavatsky ("Madame Blavatsky", 1831-1891) together with the American Henry Steel Olcott (1832-1907) founded in New York the Theosophical Society with a strong affinity to Indian religions (reincarnation). The goals of the society were "to form a nucleus of the universal brotherhood of humanity, to study comparative religion, philosophy, and science; and to investigate the mysterious laws of nature and the unknown powers in mankind" (*Compton's Interactive Encyclopedia*). For the Melbourne Secularists the most important theosophist was Annie Besant (1847-1933) who led the Theosophical Society after the death of Blavatsky and Olcott until 1933.

[203] (1833-30.1.1891). Founded with Charles Watts in 1866 the National Secular Society. On 27.6.1891 *The Liberator* announced: "Now ready (Price Sixpence) outline of Mr. Bradlaugh's Life, His Three Famous Speeches at the Bar of the House of Commons, and Mr. Symes' Article, "Bradlaugh," all in one pamphlet. Also added Mr. Bradlaugh's Portrait." See Symes' article in the *Liberator* of 7.3.1891 defending him against claims that he had renounced his atheism on his deathbed.

[204] In addition prominence was given to Captain Ingersoll's tracts (Robert Green Ingersoll, 1833-1899, US lawyer and author, known as an agnostic for lectures and books about the bible).

[205] He was a famous Enlightenment philosopher (1737-1809), wrote *The Age of Reason* (1794/96) and criticized organized religion. He was not an Atheist, but a Deist.

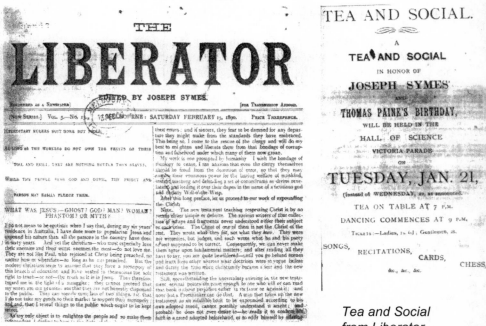

*Tea and Social
from Liberator*

Secularists were not strong numerically in Australia.[206] The leading group was the Australia Secularist Association with established groups in the major cities and individuals or small groups elsewhere.[207] The Sydney group, led by Ebenezer Skinner[208] and having William W. Collins as lecturer from England,[209] managed to publish a catechism,[210]

---

[206] For a comprehensive list of "Secular and associated organizations of unbelief in Australasia 1850-1900" see Ray Dahlitz, Secular Who's Who, pp. 10-12.

[207] Such an isolated individual was T.J. Price in Broken Hill, who requested: "Will Freethinkers, who are interested in the spread of the Gospel of Truth, kindly send me a list of intelligent people in their neighbourhood and their addresses so that I may post them *Liberators*? (*The Liberator*, 11.4.1891, p. 2411.)

[208] President of Sydney Progressive Lyceum and the Liberal Association of New South Wales. For an overview of developments at the time of building their own premises see: E. Skinner and J.G. Ross, "Sidney Jottings", *The Liberator, 18*91, p. 2297.

[209] Born 1853, he studied for the Baptist ministry but lost his faith. He came in 1885 after problems in the Sydney group, founded and edited the weekly *Freethinker* and the *New South Wales Reformer* which later merged with the *Liberator*. Moved to Christchurch, New Zealand. Died 1923. (Ray Dahlitz, Secular Who's Who, p. 7 and entry 1013).

[210] Ebenezer Skinner, *The Secularist's Guide. A Book for Young and Old*, Sydney, nd. [1890?]. The catechism's motto is taken from the Deist Thomas Paine: "The World our Country - Mankind our Brethren - to do Good our Religion".

but all failed to produce a hymn book. Secularism had no unified structure with a central organization, but consisted of loosely affiliated groups connected mainly by the reading of the *Liberator*.[211]

In the Australian Secularist movement Joseph Symes was the leading figure, and Melbourne possibly its most active group as long as things lasted. But Symes, though his outstanding position was never in doubt, was also an extremist, both in his style and in his rejection of even deism as a possibility.

Joseph Symes (1841 - 1906)

In his early years, Symes was a Christian preparing for the Methodist ministry. His doubts started when he was at the training college. After much searching, he concluded in 1872 that there is no God since there cannot be one. In 1876, he joined the British National Secular Society. He remained strongly religious, only that then Secularism became his religion. Secularism by definition is not necessarily atheistic but just agnostic, leaving it open that there may exist a God and a world beyond, though stressing that this our world and this our life is the only thing we can know about. Symes was a man of very strong convictions, so he did not leave the issue of God's possible existence open but was positive about God's non-existence, and militantly so.

For the earthly agents of the non-existing God he had no sympathy left:

> We wish to abolish christianity as the worst thing we know; we aim at converting the priests, parsons, churches, and the whole apparatus of religion into something useful, something devoted to the improvement of man's lot in life. At present, they are traders in death. And we wish to do this openly as we have ever done.[212]

Symes also held radical political views. The *Liberator* had a regular column: "Our Political Muddle", in which Symes minced no words. His views he summed up like this:

---

[211] In *The Liberator* of 21 April 1891 he sounded the call for organization: "The organization of Secularism is a question of great concern both to ourselves and the world at large. That we ought to be organised is conceded on all hands. At present we are scattered over the country, over Australasia: and the only visible bond of union is the LIBERATOR. We want this supplemented by local societies in every city and township, and all united with one central body. A union should first be sought in each colony, with the capital or other large city as the headquarters, and then there should be a federation of all the colonies under one general head. This may be done, and it should be done .... We should organise and federate for mutual protection against boycotting, newspapers, pulpit and magisterial tyranny."

[212] Joseph Symes, "Organisation", *The Liberator*, 11.4.1891.

We wish to change the government. We hate kings and queens; we are Republicans. But we do not wish to produce the change by secret means, nor yet by force. We aim at changing the public sentiment by enlightening it; so that when the people are ripe for the change it shall be affected without bloodshed.[213]

Instead of a Methodist minister, Symes became a secularist lecturer, giving his first lecture in Nelson Street Hall, Newcastle on Tyne, 17 December, 1876. His lecturing was as intense as any Methodist preaching might have been, and when the Victorian Branch of the Australasian Secular Association required a lecturer from the old country, Charles Bradlaugh recommended Joseph Symes, who arrived in Melbourne in 1884.[214] In the same year, he was elected President of the second Australasian Freethought Congress in Sydney.[215] Symes was given funds to establish a printing press and to start his own weekly paper, *The Liberator*.[216] Agnes Taylor Wilson (1866-1935) was the printer, publisher and bookseller,[217] and besides promoting the regular secularist publications, she promoted birth-control literature. Agnes Taylor Wilson was a Secularist in her own right, and she married Symes on 4 May 1893.[218]

His personality was forceful.[219] He had very good organizing abilities;[220] he was a prodigious writer and an eloquent speaker, using wit and sarcasm to the utmost. For his regular Sunday evening lectures, he chose titles like: "A few of the Deliberate Falsehoods of the Bible. With the Reasons for them,"[221] or: "The Sham Reconcilers of Faith and

---

[213] Ibid.

[214] Ray Dahlitz, *Secular Who's Who. A Bibliographical Directory of Freethinkers, Secularists, Rationalists, Humanists, and others involved in Australia's Secular Movement from 1850 onwards*, Melbourne: nd., p. 5.

[215] Ibid., entry 1045.

[216] Full set of copies 1884-1894 with a few missing in State Library of Victoria, 328 Swanston St., Melbourne, VIC 3000.

[217] Her address was 456 Bourke St, West.

[218] She helped in the production of the *Liberator* and acted as printer publisher of Symes' tracts and Charles Knowlton's birth control pamphlet, *Fruits of Philosophy*. Their only daughter was Stella Bradlaugh Symes (1894-1935). She graduated in medicine from Melbourne University and became a gynecologist and venereologist. She died when she tried to save her mother from a fire which destroyed their house (Ray Dahlitz, *Secular Who's Who*, entries 1044 and 1046).

[219] "His militant atheism and propagandist style did not endear him to all secularists but his ability, sincerity and sense of purpose place him in the top bracket of secular achievers" (*Ibid.*)

[220] Within weeks after his arrival he had set up a monthly magazine, *The Liberator*.

[221] *The Liberator*, 1890, p. 1832.

Science: A Reply to Dr. Carr's Latest,[222] and even: "Will Science Banish Atheism? A Reply to Baron Mueller."[223] He was convinced that there was nothing that could not be scientifically explained and that an increase in knowledge would drive out faith, which in other contexts he would call superstition.[224] And faith having been driven out, no one would fear death any more:

> He who believes in a hell and a horrible monster like the Christian God, may well feel horror-struck or mad in the face of death; but what ground of fear can the unbeliever have? None. He does not believe; he can not be frightened.[225]

Symes seems to have loved nothing more than controversy. After all his lectures he invited discussion and on Sundays, he preached at Queen's Wharf at 3 pm.[226] Discussion and controversy were regular features of street preaching in those days, whether Christian or Atheist. However, most controversial was his style of speaking and writing. He made good and not so good use of his wit and sarcasm, and it is astonishing that he was sued for libel only once.[227] Opponents in those days were often treated not so lightly, but he surpassed the average by far.

Symes attacked everything religious, not recoiling from what others would have called blasphemy. His tract "Phallic Worship" was a blatant example.[228]

Special attention he bestowed on the Catholic Church. A lecture on the Pope he embellished with a poem. The occasion seems to have been a report in the Melbourne newspaper *The Age* that the Belgian King Leopold had offered a residence to the Pope.

---

[222] *The Liberator*, 30.8.1890.

[223] *The Liberator*, 1890, p. 1363.

[224] In order to help in that process, Symes taught a weekly "Lyceum" class meeting in the hall of science (free for members of ASA), where he could lecture on topics like "Winds and Storms" or "Human Bones" (a lecture for which he once brought "two full skeletons, one male, one female" (30.5.1891). John Love, ASA's secretary, contributed to the increase of knowledge by a weekly shorthand class.

[225] *The Liberator*, vol. 5, no. 7 (New Series), 1890, p. 1357.

[226] After police and court action against him he had to stop preaching there, an action which even the Wharf Defence Fund could not make undone. But street preaching continued elsewhere, and there were also occasional atheist picnics. Cf. "Orders issued by the Chief Secretary that meetings of the public on the wharves of the Yarra are not to be allowed on Sundays" ("Notable Events", 4.9.1890).

[227] This was the case of Morris v. Symes in 1890 (*The Liberator*, 1890, pp. 1865, 1881.

[228] This was the rating of the *Australian Christian World* for the 6th edition: "Surpasses in blasphemy and obscenity anything we have seen or heard of".

The restive old pope had arranged to elope;
But the bobbies surrounded his den;
And he clearly foresaw, should he withdraw,
He never could get in again.

So he stifles his pain and his longings so vain
To escape and flee over to France!
Where he frets and he fumes, in the Vatican rooms
He may fiddle or fuddle or dance!

He can't get away by night or by day,
'cept by leaving his palace behind;
So he whimpers and sighs and weeps out of his eyes
To think how he is cribbed and confined.

What a fix for a god, who once proudly trod
On millions, that crawl'd in the dust!
He's now up the spout, his tricks are played out
And the bubble is ready to bust.[229]

But Protestants were not spared of his attention either. At one point, he wrote.

"Attend your church" the parson cries;
To church each fair one goes.
The old go there to close their eyes,
The young to eye their clothes.[230]

In 1890, he wrote about himself:

My friends will think that I am never out of hot water; and they are pretty correct in that.[231]

That sums up his character very well. Joseph Symes left Melbourne for Britain in 1894, where he died 3 years later. In the last issues of the *Liberator*, no reason for his departure is given, but his departure coincided with the decline and demise of organized secularist endeavour in Melbourne and Australia as a whole.[232]

The Hall of Science

The centre of Symes activities was the Hall of Science, which in the memory of Emily Booth was a big thing, but in reality it was of small

---

[229] *The Liberator*, 16.8.1890.
[230] *The Liberator*, 22.1.1888, p. 141.
[231] *Ibid.*, 9.8.1890, p. 1848.
[232] Ray Dahlitz, Secu*lar Who's Who. A Bibliographical Directory of Freethinkers, Secularists, Rationalists, Humanists, and others involved in Australia's Secular Movement from 1850 onwards*, Melbourne: nd.

proportions. Most of the time the Hall of Science was a rented room, with the locations changing over the years.[233] A building fund was collected early and a Hall of Science was established, but because of internal dissent, the money went to the Anarchist faction,[234] whom Symes, after the split and their taking of the official books and other assets, regularly called the Den of Thieves.[235] After the conflict, the Hall of Science was no longer what it had been before,[236] though, according to the *Liberator*, attendance continued between "fair and very good".

In its activities, the Hall of Science looked often like a

A report of a Sunday evening's musical section The concert on Sunday evening opened with a pianoforte duet by Messrs. Ireland and Edwards, entitled "La Brilliante," arranged by the former. Mr. Wadley followed, and succeeded in pleasing the audience with "My Sweetheart when a Boy," Scott Gatti. Miss Nimmo gave a tasteful rendering of "O fair Dove," Morgan, which suited her contralto voice to a nicety. Mr. John Walters followed with Belfe's "When other Lips," which fairly brought down the house; and in response to an enthusiastic encore, Pinsuti's beautiful song, "The Last Watch," was substituted. Mr. Walters also concluded the programme with "The Message," Blumenthal, in which the excellence of Mr. Ireland's accompaniment was particularly noticeable. Miss Sturdy, who made her second appearance on this occasion, gave "Sing, Sweet Bird," Gaaz, and "No, Never More," in response to a recall. The same artistes will appear on Sunday next, and Mr. Walters is announced to sing the serenade "O Summer Night," from Don Pasquale, Donizetti, and "My Pretty Jane," Bishop.

[233] On 24.6.1890 the Hall of Science moved to Bourke Street, in later its address was Victoria Parade.

[234] This later led to a court case, in which Symes was fined for contempt of court for entering the Hall. His side of the story is told in *The Liberator*, 28.3.1891 under the heading "A Nice State of Things": He concludes: "For about five years their conspiracy to drive me out of Melbourne has been in existence, and working night and day to accomplish its end. Three separate times the members of the gang have conspired to land me in prison. Were all this attempted against any other man the conspirators would be severely punished. But legal protection for myself is beyond possibility in the present state of Melbourne society. What then? Am I disheartened? Not one bit. I understand the human animal; and don't expect much good from him, especially when he is pious or anarchistic. He has to be encouraged in well doing; laughed at and resisted when he plays his worst pranks or runs riot under the influence of his mad passion - as the anarchists now are doing."

[235] "The anarchists and other unscrupulous persons more or less connected with the Australian Secular Association are trying every mean and cowardly trick to damage the sale of the LIBERATOR and injure the Association ... I am not at least surprised at this result of anarchy. When people openly proclaim their renunciation of all law, all sentiments, all honesty, all obligation, you must expect them to act like maniacs or utter scamps" (Symes in *The Liberator, 1887*, p. 313). The Anarchist faction was led by Frederick P. Upham (1850-1920), who had formed on 1 May 1886 the Anarchist Club within the Hall of Science. The Anarchists took the original Association's books, documents and funds, while the Symes faction retained the rented Hall of Science and the *Liberator* (Ray Dahlitz, Secu*lar Who's Who*, entry 1052).

[236] Ray Dahlitz, Secu*lar Who's Who*, p. 6.

church, and Symes used church terminology. The key function was the Sunday evening "service", when the (non-) faithful gathered for a liturgy of song and poetry (6.30 - 7.00 pm, later one full hour), followed by a lecture (Symes did not call it a sermon).[237] Sunday afternoon was reserved for outreach (street propaganda), and once Symes even started a class for atheist propaganda. There was also, at least at times, a regular Sunday School. Highlight of the week were the socials with lots of solos, cards and chess playing and dancing up to late. Part of the Hall of Science was the Lyceum which featured the two classes of Science (Symes) and shorthand (John Love[238]). There was a lending library and the secretary was in attendance for quite a number of hours every week.[239] In addition, there were committee meetings, picnics,[240] birthday socials, special lecturers with guest speakers, and special collections.[241] As in a Christian church, women played a great role in providing the tea and the music, but though Symes was much in favour of women's rights, I found no woman giving lectures. In common with Christian churches were regular invitations to members to get more involved (and occasional complaints that they did not).

Booth and Symes

In her memories, Emily Langworthy-Booth creates a picture of her father's discussions with Symes, which does not fully match historical

---

[237] He differed from Christian preachers by inviting critical response, but then his was a religion of reason. Some of his topics were: "Royalty Exhibiting its Mud: Or the Card-Sharper Prince and the Papers" (21.6.1891); "Religious Conversion: Its Philosophy Explained, its Blunders Exposed" (28.6.1891); "Marriage: Its Drawbacks and the Necessity for Reform" (12.1.1889) followed the next Sunday by: "The Disgusting and Tyrannous Relations of Catholic Priests to Women, and their Revived Crusade against Mixed Marriages". On Sunday, 24th June, the topic was: "The Paltry Character of God's Female Friends, or Bible Women Contrasted with the Great and Good of Their Sex".

[238] For Love see entry 1022 in Ray Dahlitz, Secular Who's Who: "Secularist, atheist. Supporter of Joseph Symes, secretary of ASA [Australasian Secular Association], during the time of the factional split and fight for control of the Melbourne Hall of Science".

[239] A typical schedule from the early days was: Tuesday night: Council Meeting, Wednesday night: Members' Dancing Class (8-10.30), Thursday night: Choir Practice (8-10), Friday night: Symes' Science class (8-9.00) Shorthand (John Love, 9-10.00), The Liberator, 1891, p. 2443.

[240] "Propagandist Picnic to Mitcham. Vans will start from the Hall of Science at 11 o'clock sharp. Mr. Joseph Symes will speak on the Opening of Libraries and Museums on Sundays. Discussion invited (The Liberator, 1890, p. 1364).

[241] Building Fund, Wharf Defence Fund, collection to honour Charles Bradlaugh.

reality. She writes that Symes had challenged all the ministers of Melbourne to public debate and since nobody accepted, Booth had ventured to defend the faith. Then, for quite a number of weeks, the two would discuss publicly, with up to 1200 people paying 1 shilling to listen to the debates in the Hall of Science.[242]

Some of what she reports is correct. Symes' Hall of Science existed, there were discussions and entry fees,[243] but all was much less spectacular. Symes challenged almost everyone to debate and at least two full-scale public debates with equal terms for both sides took place. The first took place in 1884 between him and Rev D.M. Berry, the chaplain to the Bishop of Melbourne.[244] The other public debate took place between Symes and Isaac Selby, who had been an active participant and lecturer in the Hall of Science[245] and then reconverted to Christianity. Therefore, Symes challenged him to a public debate.[246] The six nights' debate took place in the Temperance Hall and the proceedings were verbatim recorded by a secretary from each side, and published after approval by Symes and Selby.[247] The topic of the first three evenings was "Is Christian Theism More Rational than Atheistic Secularism? - Mr. Selby to affirm. Mr Symes to Deny." The topic of the last three evenings was "Is the New Testament Jesus a Myth? - Mr Symes to Affirm. Mr Selby to Deny". Every evening the affirming speaker would open the discussion with a 30 minutes speech, after that his opponent could reply for 15 minutes and so on.

---

[242] Harry Langworthy, *The Life of Joseph Booth*, p. 23. – This note refers to the real lectures: "Jos Symes lectures in the New Hall of Science, Vic Parade. 'A Few of the Deliberate Falsehoods of the Bible; With the Reasons for them.' Doors open 6.30, Lecture 7.30. Good musical programme prior to Lecture. Front seats 1 s, back seats 6 d (*The Liberator*, 1890, p. 1832).

[243] In the Hall of Science the entry fees was 1 sh for the front seats, 6d for the back seats.

[244] Manuscript S204 L518 (V.3) in the State Library of Victoria: "Is it rational to believe that Jesus rose from the dead? Debate between Mr. Joseph Symes and Rev. D.M. Berry, nd., 48 pp.

[245] "We helped him as we could but he was none of us."

[246] *The Liberator*, 23.8.90, p. 1881.

[247] Both praised John Love, the secretary of the Hall of Science, for his accurate work. The report (242 [small] pages) was published by The Austral Publishing Company, 528 Elizabeth Street, in 1892 as: *Selby and Symes Debate. A Full Report of the Six Nights' Debate held in the Temperance Hall, Melbourne, in the months of August and September, 1892 between Joseph Symes, President and Lecturer of the Australasian Secular Association and Isaac Selby, Christian Minister*.

Those debates were rare, and there is no evidence that there was a Symes vs Booth debate of that type.[248] Neither is there any support for an attendance of up to 1200, as Emily remembers:

> Every Sunday evening up to 1200 people paid one shilling each to pack the Hall of Science to hear the Atheist and the Christian debate.[249]

The various Halls of Science would not accommodate that many.[250] The only attendance figure I found, being more precise than "fair, good, very good, or many in spite of late announcement", was 70 couples at a birthday celebration for Thomas Pane and Joseph Symes in 1888, before the Anarchists split off from the Hall of Science,[251] and judging from the details which are given about the activities of the Hall of Science I conclude that the adult congregation was definitely less than 200.[252] This estimate can be corroborated by the size of the new Hall of Science, Victoria Parade no. 9.[253] It was situated behind the home of Mrs Mary McDonald on a plot which measured 40x40 ft, of which at most about 30x25 ft (c. 9x7 m) may have been occupied by the Hall of Science.[254] Joseph Symes also lived on the plot.[255] The small scale of the Halls of Sciences is supported by the fact that the printing press was "idle a large part of its time".[256]

---

[248] Nothing was published, and the *Liberator* does not record anything. Symes' lectures are usually recorded and that record does not leave any space for extended formal discussion with Booth.

[249] Harry Langworthy, *The Life of Joseph Booth*, p. 23.

[250] In 1888 the Hall of Science moved from Burke St E to Collins St W (*The Liberator, 1*888, p. 313).

[251] "The Hall was prettily decorated .... about 70 couples present" (*The Liberator*, 1888, 169). As with other dances it seems to have been more difficult to attract the ladies. Their entrance fees were regularly less than what men would pay.

[252] This estimate may well be on the higher side, taking into account an outside report quoted in the *Liberator* (1888, p. 49): "Sunday Night with the Freethinkers ... He is one lecturer, with a by no means large audience - more than half of whom are certainly not infidels".

[253] "As to the land in Victoria Parade, we have taken possession of that, and mean to keep it. We'll build there" (*The Liberator, 1*888, p. 364).

[254] The whole bloc is now part of St. Vincent's Hospital. It is true that a New Hall of Science was built after the Anarchistic controversy which had reduced their membership. But Symes' claim that attendance continued to be good after the controversy and the *Liberator* give no evidence that the old rented Hall was bigger. It was taken over by the YMCA (*The Liberator, 1*888, p. 341).

[255] In the *Melbourne Directory Sands and McDougall* of 1890 two Joseph Symes are entered, one living in Victoria Parade, the other in 104 High St, Pra.

[256] *The Liberator, 1*888, p. 441. On 4 January 1890 readers were admonished: "All Freethinkers should support their own LIBERATOR PRESS. Send in all the printing jobs you can.

Though Emily's perception of Booth' debates with Symes has to be downsized considerably, they did take place, and beside reminiscences there is local evidence. In one of the regular reports from Brighton Baptist Church published in the denomination's monthly, Booth's evangelistic band is mentioned, and another describes the missionary work on Queen's Wharf:

> On Sunday mornings, at 11, on Flinders Street wharf, a service is held, at which a collection is taken to feed the hungry. At 2.30 debates with and addresses to secularists, also Gospel preaching. At 7.30, he attends the secularists' meeting at the Hall of Science, to contend for the faith. Some of this work he is personally well fitted for. Originally an atheist, he knows their flimsy arguments and can meet them adroitly.[257]

Queen's Wharf, photographed by J.W. Lindt
(La Trobe Picture Collection, State Library of Victoria)

This suggests that Booth, together with others from his church, often spent Sunday afternoon at Queen's Wharf preaching, and this may well have brought him into contact with the Secularists' preaching there at the same time. In the evening he could then attend the Secularists'

---

[257] "Mixed News," *The Baptist Freeman*, Oct 1889, p. 138.

evening service and use the opportunity of discussion offered to present the Christian message contradicting the Secularists' teaching, an effort to which the fact that he had once been an atheist and knew their literature and arguments lent credibility, at least as much credibility as the fact that Symes had been a Methodist preacher lent credibility to his conversion to Secularism. Booth's interaction with Symes in these meetings is recorded once in the *Liberator*:

> Mr. Symes' subject was: "Why are People Religious, and what does it Bring to Them?" and Mr. Booth appeared as usual to oppose, and said that he always despised lecturers who made a lot of ribald statements. He was religious that he was deeply convinced that the weight of evidence was on the side of the religious man. Facts did not agree with the lecturer's statement that where knowledge came in religion went out. He (Mr. Booth) always felt considerably annoyed when he came on that platform, for he had only 10 minutes in which to reply to a lecture of 40 minutes' duration.
>
> Mr. Symes said that he thought that when Mr. Booth came on the platform, instead of wasting his time complaining that he had only 10 minutes, he should get to work with what he had. He had talked about ribaldry. If a man is to be honest he must laugh at what appears to him to be laughable. Mr. Booth had said that these were important matters. He (Mr. Symes) had treated them as such, and it was only after the argument that he indulged in the laugh. (Applause)
>
> [signed] Dagon[258]

This is the only reference in the *Liberator* to Booth's activities,[259] but it is significant as it describes a repeated activity. This would match Booth's assessment:

> To my surprise and relief, I found a great deal of hearty encouragement from a goodly number and bitterness from a few. For several years, this became my training college and I got to know my man and was able to shatter some of his rash positions and pretences.[260]

Though Symes remained unconverted just as much as Booth, from Booth's side it was foremost a missionary effort, an outcrop of street preaching, though not devoid of intellectual challenge. If Booth's activities had any measurable effect on the listener of the debating, cannot be assessed from the available sources. Nevertheless, the effort

---

[258] *The Liberator, 18*91, p. 2297 (21.2.1891).

[259] Since I had only three days to follow Booth's contacts with the Secularists, there is the possibility that I overlooked a reference. But I looked carefully through the relevant issues, and did find several references to Booth, but in all other cases to General Booth of the Salvation Army whom Symes disliked wholeheartedly.

[260] Harry Langworthy, *The Life of Joseph Booth*, p. 23. This is a quote with no source indicated, possibly from "Into Africa" by Emily Langworthy-Booth.

shows definitely a Booth who was willing to stand up for his convictions and be counted, an attitude that would repeat itself in Africa in his political convictions, which equally showed in his missionary effort.[261]

From the evidence available in Melbourne a picture emerges of Booth's convictions and personality matching very well that which emerges from his time in Malawi: The strong convictions are there, the willingness to present them forcefully, too. Only for that side of his character that made it difficult for him to cooperate over time with the same people there is no real evidence. He got on well with the people of his congregation, but it could be argued that his time in Melbourne (October 1887 to May 1891) was too short for any real assessment. The fact remains that he moved frequently, just as settlers at the frontier were ever willing to move forward to a place with perceivably better land and opportunities.[262]

7. The missionary call

It is quite possible that, like the Tabernacle Baptists in London, the Auckland Tabernacle had a strong missionary commitment. Thomas' Spurgeon's father's Metropolitan Tabernacle and A.G. Brown's West London Tabernacle had equally a strong commitment, but not much towards their old established denominational mission, the Baptist Missionary Society (BMS), founded by William Carey in 1792[263] and working in Bangladesh, then called India.[264] These "Tabernacle" churches directed their foreign mission involvement to the interdenominational faith missions instead, which were more akin to their spirituality and

---

[261] I suspect that were more sources available, more of his social and political "progressive" views could be documented for his Melbourne years, not only the conviction of human equality. Perhaps some of those motions should be clarified as Christian rather than as progressive, since for example William Carey, whom Booth saw as his shining example, had expressed them in print already in 1792.

[262] This interpretation was first suggested to me in a discussion after a Departmental Seminar, and I also found this settler attitude reflected in the history of the Seventh Day Baptists (Don A. Sanford, *A Choosing People: The History of Seventh Day Baptists*, Nashville: Broadman, 1992).

[263] Carey outlined his theology of missions and his plan for action in: William Carey, *An Enquiry into the Obligations of Christians, to Use Means for the Conversion of the Heathens. In which the religious state of the different nations of the world, the success of former undertakings and the practicability of further undertakings, are considered*, Leicester 1792.

[264] Victorian Baptists were to support the same society. In the annual assembly 1891 foreign mission reports were only from the BMS in India (*The Victorian Baptist*, 1891, p. 106-107).

theology. Brown's West London Tabernacle supported the Baptist Missionary Society only after his death,[265] and Charles Haddon Spurgeon had a very close relationship to the first interdenominational Missionary Training Institute (The East London Training Institute for Evangelists at Home and Abroad)[266] and their founders Fanny and Grattan Guinness.[267] There was also a strong relationship between the "ELTI" and Spurgeon's Pastors' College, which supplied a good number of pastors to Baptist congregations in Australia.[268] Both operated on the premise that personality and spirituality are the basis for theological education, not Latin, Greek and a good social background, and that a theological school should train people competent to do the job.[269] This means that the time in Auckland may have given Booth already the broad vision of foreign missions, and if not that, the context there provided him with a spiritually vibrant framework within which to experience the call and put it into reality.

Brighton Church was, as it was usual for Victorian Baptists in those years, interested in foreign missions, but the interest was stronger than average, and Stephen Howard, the pastor, was in the forefront of this interest. As with all Victorian Baptists, the congregation's missionary interest was first of all directed to "India", where they had their own area of the traditional Baptist Missionary Society mission field with Mymensing as centre and work being most successful among—but not

---

[265] (George E. Page, A.G.B., *The Story of the Life and Work of Archibald Geikie Brown*, London 1944)

[266] This ELTI is the mother of all modern bible schools. See Klaus Fiedler, "Aspects of the Early History of the Bible School Movement", in Festschrift Donald Mooreland, ed. by Marthinus W. Praetorius: *The Secret of Faith. In Your Heart - In Your Mouth*, Heverlee/Leuven 1992, pp. 62-77. Reprinted in: Klaus Fiedler, *Conflicted Power in Malawian Christianity: Essays Missionary and Evangelical from Malawi*, Mzuzu: Mzuni Press, 2015. pp. 240-258.

[267] Michelle Guinness, *The Guinness Legend*, London: Hodder and Stoughton, 1990, pp. 48ff.

[268] In 1891 the ministers selected for Collins Street and Albert Street, the two Baptist congregations of central Melbourne, Hill and Ellis, were both graduates of Spurgeon's Pastors' College (*The Victorian Baptist*, April 1891, p. 63).

[269] Spurgeon, though, trained men only. The two schools visited each other and shared activities. When Spurgeon invited the East London Training Institute for a sports competition, he stipulated that, except Fanny Guinness, only men should come. Lucy Guinness noted in her dairy "with great glee that Mama should be the only female member of the Harley [ELTI] party, but Mama, who was not daunted by anyone, even the most famous preacher in England, took five female friends with her including her two daughters. Never in her life, Lucy claimed, has she heard such a deafening noise as the sound of all those young men eating and talking! (Michelle Guinness, *The Guinness Legend*, London/Sydney/Auckland/ Toronto: Hodder and Stoughton, 1990, p. 140)

confined to—the Gwaru, one of "the tribes".[270] The first missionary from Brighton to leave for the mission field in Booth's time was Miss E. Chambers, daughter of one of the deacons and "one of our most devoted church workers" who went to India,[271] and an Indian "assistant missionary", Boboo Joy Nath Chowdry, was invited to canvass support for the work there.[272]

The congregation's broad foreign missions interest was reflected in the congregation's prayer meetings.

> In addition to the usual collecting of subscriptions undertaken by the Mission Committee, other means of stirring up and sharing interest in the work have been used. Letters from India and Africa, and an occasional letter from China, as they are received by different members, are read at our Wednesday evening prayer meeting.[273]

The next member to leave for the mission field was Marie Box. Together with three other single women who had joined the China Inland Mission, she was given a farewell meeting in her church,[274] and the *Victorian Freeman*[275] reported for some time on the ladies' progress.

The next two members of the congregation who decided to become missionaries were the Booths and the congregation extended their support to them as well, symbolically expressed in organizing a farewell meeting for them. Brighton, unlike Auckland, was not of the Tabernacle type, but since Baptist church polity allows each congregation considerable (in theory: full) independence, Brighton, like the other congregations, could extend its missionary interests beyond the denominational mission.[276]

---

[270] A number of ethnic groups in the "tribal areas" of the mountains of India responded enthusiastically to the preaching of the Gospel.

[271] *The Victorian Baptist*, June 1891, p. 112.

[272] He had been invited by the Baptists of Victoria for this purpose (*The Victorian Baptist*, 2/1893, p. 45). His successor was a Victorian Baptist.

[273] *The Victorian Baptist*, 4/1894, p. 88.

[274] Such "farewell meetings" took the place of what in other missionary traditions would have been "commissioning meetings", but since the faith missionaries were members of the mission and not its employees, they could not be commissioned; but a farewell meeting, though of no binding character, was usually a meeting also to express the willingness to pray for the missionary and to give some financial support.

[275] The monthly Baptist journal, till the end of 1889 *The Victorian Freeman*, then *The Victorian Baptist*.

[276] In an incomplete list these missionaries who did not serve with the BMS in India are found: Mr. and Mrs. O. Deeath (Aberdeen St) to Nyasaland, Mrs and Miss Henry (Aberdeen St) to Ceylon, Mr Purdy (Ballarat) to New Hebrides, Mr and Mrs H.W. Long (Malden) to

From the evidence available, it is quite possible that the first precise call was Mary Jane Booth's dream that a messenger from China was calling her or them. If dreams are interpreted as reflections of subconscious realities, this dream, couched as it was in biblical imagery,[277] shows that she had by then reached a point where she was willing to become a missionary, and the discussion with her husband, also with good biblical precedent,[278] decided the issue in principle for both of them.[279] Some time after that the "atheist's call" gave the decision a new poignancy (or the other way round?), and then the sale of the milk palace partnership sealed the deal.

Mission: yes, but why interdenominational and industrial?

In May 1891 Joseph Booth went to Britain to find the sphere of their future missionary work, but with the refusals leaving no options open, he would not give up anyhow, as that would not have been in keeping with his character.[280] His particular choice of missionary approach can be explained thus:

1   From his spiritual background in Auckland and Melbourne an interdenominational faith mission would have been the regular option, a denominational Baptist mission the unusual option.

2   His spiritual background was of an innovative type. So to choose a new approach, that of an industrial mission, was not so strange.

Zambezi Industrial Mission, Miss Bellen and Miss Box to South Africa, Messrs. E. Barber, W. Seaman, H. Kitchen and others to China Inland Mission, Miss R. Hinton to Poona Mission, the daughters of Dr. D.S. MacColl, one to India, one to China, the two daughters of Mr. F. Harley, to the Sudan Mission (F.J. Wilkin, *Baptists in Victoria. Our First Century 1838-1938*, Melbourne 1939, p. 120).

[277] And when they had come opposite Mysia, they attempted to go into Bithynia, but the Spirit of Jesus did not allow them; so, passing by Mysia, they went down to Troas. And a vision appeared to Paul in the night: a man of Macedonia was standing beseeching him and saying, "Come over to Macedonia and help us" (Acts 16:7-10, RSV).

[278] "And when he had seen the vision, immediately we sought to go on into Macedonia, concluding that God had called us to preach the gospel to them" (Acts 16:10, RSV).

[279] That Joseph agreed so quickly means that both had been thinking of becoming missionaries.

[280] This sequence is how it appears from the evidence, but I can imagine that Booth had developed some of his industrial mission ideas already before the trip to London, and then his request was to join China Inland Mission, London Missionary Society or Baptist Missionary Society on his own term, in form of an industrial mission. His conversation with the BMS representative makes this appear possible.

3   As a Baptist, he did not need any ordination, and as a businessman, why should he not use means and methods from that side of life for the expansion of the Kingdom?

Booth's eschatology was, as could be assumed from his background, closely tied to missiology. The Booths shared many of the ideas of the Holiness Movement, a renewal which started in 1835 without being tied to a specific eschatology, but which by 1870 had almost completely changed from postmillennial to premillennial eschatology.[281] Premillennial missiology took its departure point from Matthew 24:14 where Jesus taught that the moment of his second coming would depend on the gospel having been preached everywhere.[282] In order to bring back the king, it was top priority to reach those who had never heard the message, not even once. To reach the unreached was the very reason for the existence of the faith missions as a new movement,[283] and in his planning Booth produced nothing unusual. He wanted to reach the unreached parts of Africa, and interdenominational missions were a frequently employed means to achieve that.[284] Since the message was urgent, the faith missions did not require ordination of their missionaries and could recruit candidates who would have been unacceptable to classical missions. They could also employ unusual visions and both the idea of a chain of mission stations across

---

[281] For a discussion of faith mission eschatology in the context of the Prophetic Movement see Klaus Fiedler, *The Story of Faith Missions. From Hudson Taylor to Present Day Africa*, Oxford/Akropong/Buenos Aires, Irvine, New Delhi: Regnum Books International, ²1995(1994), pp. 272-291. See also: Klaus Fiedler, "Shifts in Eschatology - Shifts in Missiology", in: Jochen Eber (ed.), *Hope does not Disappoint. Studies in Eschatology. Essays from Different Contexts*, Wheaton: World Evangelical Fellowship – Theological Commission, Bangalore: Theological Book Trust, 2001. See also http://www.worldevangeli cal. org/cdresourcelib.html. Reprinted as Klaus Fiedler, *Conflicted Power in Malawian Christianity: Essays Missionary and Evangelical from Malawi*, Mzuzu: Mzuni Press, 2015, pp. 260-280

[282] "And this gospel of the kingdom will be preached in the whole world as a testimony to all nations, and then the end will come" (NIV).

[283] Klaus Fiedler, *The Story of Faith Missions*, pp. 125ff.

[284] The first faith mission in Africa was Fanny Guinness' Livingstone Inland Mission, founded in 1878 (see Fanny Guinness, *The New World of Central Africa. With a History of the First Christian Mission on the Congo*, London 1890, pp. 173ff.) More important faith missions in Africa were Africa Inland Mission (1895), Sudan Interior Mission (1902) and Sudan United Mission (1904). The other faith mission to work in Malawi besides those started by Joseph Booth was the South Africa General Mission (later named Africa Evangelical Fellowship), which worked in the southern tip of Malawi and later formed with the churches of the Nyasa Industrial Mission the Africa Evangelical Church (now Evangelical Church of Malawi).

THE CHAIN IN THE STRATEGY OF THE EARLY FAITH MISSIONS

Abbreviations:
AIM: Africa Inland Mission
CMA: Christian and Missionary Alliance
SIM: Sudan Interior Mission
SPM: Sudan Pioneer Mission
SUM: Sudan United Mission

wide areas[285] and of self-supporting industrial missions[286] was current in the faith missions of those days.[287]

If the Booths, so to say, swam in the strong flow of the missionary current of the revival to which they spiritually belonged, what was special about *their* concepts? Not so much in terms of content, but it was special that they did all somewhat at the edge. They were too old, they had no training at all, their vision of industrial mission was much grander, and they would be able to finance some of the beginnings with their own money. Booth's radical personality, combined with a strong upward movement in the spiritual situation, made this more extreme version of otherwise "regular" concepts possible, though, as the future would show, not all necessarily executable.[288]

---

[285] For overview and details: Klaus Fiedler, *The Story of Faith Missions*, pp. 73-78.

[286] Among the Baptists, William Carey was the first to propagate the industrial mission idea (*Enquiry*, pp. 73-74) and Booth formulated it in a similar way. But it may be that he had not gleaned the concept directly from Carey, but from the Methodist William Taylor, who was a very vocal proponent of the idea and who had strong support in the Baptist Association of Victoria and in the *Missionary Review of the World*, the innovative evangelical missiological journal in which Booth would soon publish his own industrial mission concept.

[287] It was employed or attempted by the Christian Missionary Alliance in Zaire, Sudan Interior Mission in Nigeria, Africa Inland Mission in Kenya - but Nyasa Industrial Mission and Zambezi Industrial Mission, until the coffee blight of 1929, were the only really viable industrial faith missions. For Zambezi Industrial Mission see: *The Zambezi Mission. Missionaries Support Themselves for Thirty Years*, np, nd [1930].

[288] The same enthusiasm was shared by the Swiss Héli Chatelin. Like Booth he combined the ideas of a chain of mission stations and of self-supporting industrial missions, planning to extend the work from central Angola towards Katanga. He expected the first station to

A time of ferment and renewal

Around Booth's time in Brighton, the Baptists in Victoria had good times. Numbers were growing everywhere, the denomination was expanding. In this process, influences from the Holiness Revival played a major role. The heroes of the faith, as reflected in the columns of the Baptist monthly were Charles Haddon Spurgeon (the most famous preacher of his days),[289] William Booth (Salvation Army),[290] Thomas Barnardo (Founder of the famous children's homes in London's East End),[291] Hudson Taylor (the founder of the China Inland Mission),[292] George Müller (Brethren preacher and founder of the famous orphanages in Bristol[293] - who visited Victoria in 1888)[294] - all closely related to the Holiness Revival. In addition, the denominational journal treated increasingly holiness topics like the "deeper Christian life." Its major institutional expression was the annual Geelong Conference,[295] patterned after the Keswick Conference,[296] the centre of the Holiness

---

earn enough in a few years to establish a new station further east (Philafrican Liberators' League [ed.], "The First Expedition Successful", New York, 1897 in Alida Chatelin [ed.], *Les rapports de la Mission Philafricain 1898-1905*, Lausanne, nd.) Like Booth, he got his calculations wrong, and like Booth he laid the foundation for a (regular) mission and a church, which exists still today.

[289] *The Victorian Freeman*, February 1899, contains a full page portrait of Spurgeon.

[290] Glenn K. Horridge, *The Salvation Army: Origins and Early Days: 1865-1900*. Godalming: Ammonite Books, 1993.

[291] David E. Fessenden, *Father to Nobody's Children: The Life of Thomas J. Barnardo*, Halesowen: Christian Literature Crusade, 1995.

[292] "The Rev. J. Hudson Taylor has been lifting on the shoulders of his own strong faith many of the Lord's people to a loftier altitude. Whatever benefit he may be securing to the China Inland Mission, which he so ably manages, he certainly has brought personal blessings to his hearers, in unfolding to them the wonderful possibilities open to him that believeth" (*The Victorian Baptist*, October 1890, p. 147).

[293] George Müller also made famous the "faith principle" of financial support, developed first by Anthony Norris Groves, the first Brethren missionary in 1828. Hudson Taylor learnt it from George Müller. See: George Müller, *A Narrative of some of the Lord's Dealings with George Müller Written by Himself*, London,[9] 1895 ([1]1837). For a thorough study of Anthony Norris Groves see: Robert Bernard Dann, *The Primitivist Missiology of Anthony Norris Groves: A Radical Influence on Nineteenth-Century Protestant Mission*, Victoria, BC: Trafford, 2007.

[294] He preached in Albert Street Baptist Church on Sunday evening, 11 December (*The Victorian Freeman*, Dec. 1887, p. 4).

[295] Geelong is about an hour south west of Melbourne.

[296] Arthur T. Pierson, *The Keswick Movement in Precept and Practice*, New York/London 1903; John Ch. Pollock, *The Keswick Story - The Authorized History of the Keswick Convention*, Chicago: Moody, 1964.

Movement in Britain. [297] The first Australian Keswick Conference took place in Geelong 15-17 September 1891. In the *Victorian Baptist* this was announced:

> Of late years, a deep and spreading interest has been felt throughout the world upon the subject of Holiness, and Australasia has felt the impact of that wave ... Several of our ministers are to take part in the proceedings, and over the whole a 'Keswick' man, who understands the methods of the renowned conclave, will preside - the Rev. G.C. Grubb, M.A. We trust that many Baptists will attend.[298]

The conference was well attended, and it moved people indeed. This is reflected in a rebuttal of slanderous press reports:

> The untrustworthiness of newspaper reports was never more signally illustrated than in those which have been circulated respecting the Geelong Convention. The meetings have been represented as scenes of wild delirium, culminating in one in which men and women lost all control of themselves. Nothing could be more outrageous than such statements. The meetings were meetings of gladness, which could not be disguised, but they were characterised by sobriety from first to last. The facts of the missionary meeting are that, after addresses, intensely interesting and moving, Mr. Grubb, who at first thought of dismissing the meeting without any immediate appeal, asked for volunteers for mission service, and about fifty men and women responded; then he quietly asked for the means to send these volunteers, and just as quietly promises were handed in, which included *two* of property. Others gave their jewellery, consisting of watches, rings, brooches, etc., but the whole was done without solicitation and in great quietness - though not without joyfulness. The delirium of the occasion was in the imagination of the newspaper reporters and nowhere else.[299]

At the same time, premillennial eschatology began to replace the original postmillennial theology,[300] which for William Carey had been an unquestioned part of his missiology,[301] but which most of the Holiness

---

[297] For the movement as a whole see Melvin Dieter, *The Holiness Revival of the Nineteenth Century*, Metuchen: Scarecrow 1980; Charles Edwin Jones, *A Guide to the Study of the Holiness Movement*, Metuchen: Scarecrow 1974.

[298] *The Victorian Baptist*, August 1891, p. 144.

[299] *Ibid.*, October 1891, p. 183 (full quote).

[300] Postmillennialism did not go out unchallenged: "Their argument is that sin and iniquity were never more powerful than now, though Christian activity is greater than ever, and that the time has come when the Lord must appear in person to gather out from the prevailing wickedness his hard-pressed and sorely-tempted followers, and take them up with Him into the air. The dead in Christ will be translated first and then the living saints" (*The Victorian Baptist*, March 1891).

[301] William Carey, *An Enquiry into the Obligations of Christians to Use Means for the Conversion of the Heathens*, Leicester 1792, pp. 77-79.

Revival and all the faith missions had discarded.[302] Brighton was exposed to premillennial teaching, when Rev G.W. Gillings in 1887 paid four visits to Brighton "to examine the premillennial advent". It is reported that he spoke "as one having authority".[303] In America and Britain, the premillennial eschatology found its expression in "Prophetic Conferences", during which the evidence for the premillennial advent of Christ was examined and the "signs of the times" were used to interpret history and future in the light of the bible.[304] In Victoria, these conferences took place at Ballarat.[305] The issue was also discussed at conferences of the Baptist Association in Victoria[306] and in the denominational paper.[307]

In organizational terms the spread of the Christian Endeavour Movement meant much progress, since by this the youth of the church were taken seriously as a distinct group,[308] and in addition, it opened,

---

[302] The Restoration Revival remained divided. The Brethren were the most devoted premillennialists but of the Churches of Christ only a quarter left the original Postmillennialism for Premillennialism (Klaus Fiedler, Conflicted Power in Malawian Christianity: Essays Missionary and Evangelical from Malawi, Mzuzu: Mzuni Press, 2015 pp. 300-321).

[303] The Victorian Freeman, June 1887. From this note and other evidence I conclude that Brighton congregation, or at least its leadership and majority, had accepted premillennialism at the time when the Booths joined, who in turn came from Auckland Baptist Tabernacle, a clearly premillennial congregation.

[304] A good example of the literature produced is Grattan Guinness, Light for the Last Days. A Study Historical and Prophetical, London 1886; ²1917. Grattan Guinness was at the same time a leader in the faith mission movement, (co-)founder of the first bible school, and a leader in the Prophetic Movement. His second marriage to Grace Hurditch in the Mile End Assembly Hall, London, on 17 March 1887, was reported in the Victorian Freeman.

[305] The Victorian Freeman, January 1888, p. 20. The Prophetic Conference "was largely attended".

[306] C. W. Walroud read a paper at a half-yearly meeting of the association titled: "The Postmillennial Advent of the Lord Jesus Christ" (The Victorian Freeman, July 1888, pp. 123-124).

[307] For example J.W. Gillings, "Our Lord's Interest in His Second Coming" (The Victorian Baptist, 1840, p. 39).

[308] In 1892 there were already 175 Christian Endeavour Societies in Victoria (The Victorian Baptist, 1892, p. 173).

true to its Holiness background, new venues for women's advancement in leadership.

Joseph and Emily Booth, 1893

All those and possibly other elements combined to create an atmosphere of spiritual progress which had room for new ideas to flourish,[309] and as long as the boom lasted and the banks had not crashed, there was also enough money to finance such an expansion, ranging from improving existing church buildings like in Brighton via establishing Christian Endeavour groups and a Theological College to holding major conferences. Booth's intended Central Africa mission was one of those many advances, but when it began to be realized, the financial crisis hit it almost immediately.

Joseph Booth came back from London; the tickets were booked for the steamer, and three weeks before the departure date Mary Jane Booth died of pneumonia. Her husband decided not to delay the departure, and that is probably what Mrs Booth had wanted. Joseph Booth intended to leave Edward and Emily in London, Emily for school and Edward for missionary training, which he received at the East London Training Institute of Fanny and Grattan Guineas. Before she died, Mary Jane Booth made her husband promise never to force little Emily from him.[310] This promise in mind he took her first to South Africa and then to Malawi.[311]

Zambezi Industrial Mission and Nyasa Industrial Mission

Before Booth left, he established something like an Australian Home

---

[309] The period of rapid progress came to an end at the turn of the century

[310] Harry Langworthy, *The Life of Joseph Booth*, p. 25.

[311] She only stayed a few years, and never again lived with her father for any extended period. Later in her life she wrote the manuscript "Into Africa with Father", published in an abbreviated version as: Emily Booth-Langworthy, *This Africa was Mine*, Stirling Tract Enterprises, 1950. In Malawi she was very fond of John Chilembwe, who often looked after her when her father was away, nursed her when sick and probably once saved her life.

Council of the interdenominational mission to be first under the name of East African Industrial Mission, then as the Australian Auxiliary of the Zambezi Industrial Mission.[312] On this information is still very scanty, but Rev Howard was a member of it. Booth found support in Britain through Robert Caldwell, which led to the establishment of the first industrial mission at Mitsidi.[313] While establishing Mitsidi for the Zambezi Industrial Mission, Booth in 1893 started at Likhubula a second mission station for Australian missionaries.[314] The leading missionary couple there seems to have been Oliver and Mrs Deeath, Victorian Baptists from Aberdeen Street congregation in Melbourne; Mr and Mrs H.W. Long of Malden are also mentioned in the Victorian Baptist records. Within a short period tensions were developing between Booth and the missionaries of both Mitsidi and Likhubula, which led to the separate incorporation of the two missions. Mitsidi became the base for the larger Zambezi Industrial Mission[315] and Likhubula[316] the beginning of the smaller Nyasa Industrial Mission.[317] By 1896, Booth had stopped to play a role in either of the missions[318] and had started in 1895 the Baptist Industrial Mission of Scotland.[319]

Melbourne's economics crises

The collapse of the land boom

While Booth was in Melbourne, it became obvious that the land boom

---

[312] Harry Langworthy, *The Life of Joseph Booth*, 69.

[313] The original Mitsidi Mission was in the area of what is now Sanjika Palace of the President close to Blantyre. A new mission was built outside the fence, but the original cemetery remains within the Sanjika boundary.

[314] See also: *A Short History of Africa Evangelical Fellowship in Malawi from 1900 to 1989*, np., nd., 3 pp. (copy at Baptist Seminary, Lilongwe).

[315] Today Zambezi Evangelical Church.

[316] The centre of the mission later moved to Ntambanyama. For a major leader see: *Pastor Charles Bonongwe. Chosen, Called and Faithful*, nd.

[317] Harry Langworthy, *The Life of Joseph Booth*, pp. 69-70

[318] For the story of the establishment with much detail see Langworthy, *The Life of Joseph Booth*, pp. 31-70.

[319] Harry Langworthy, *The Life of Joseph Booth*, 70-73. The first mission was at Gowa in Central Malawi. It was not an official mission of the Scottish Baptists, but individual Scottish Baptist supported it. In the 1920s the mission declined and was in 1929 handed over to the British Church of Christ who had already started missionary work in Southern Malawi in 1907 (Ernest Gray, *The Early History of the Church of Christ Missionary Work in Nyasaland, Central Africa, 1907-1930*, Church of Christ Historical Society Occasional Paper No. 1 [Cambridge, 1981].

had collapsed, and observers with more than a superficial understanding were not unhappy about that. The Baptist denominational journal commented:

> The Land Boom appears to have collapsed - we hope finally, for it was a social epidemic, well named a "fever", and as disastrous to healthful commercial life as its name suggests. We must sincerely commiserate the many whose worst experience is not disappointment in the large prospective gains. Alas! Some are losing the accumulations of many years of honest toil, in legitimate paths of industry. Revelations are being made of shameful sacrifices of principle in the unhallowed greed for gold, which makes us blush for the Christian name. Poverty, with honour, were infinitely preferable to the disclosures, which are now being made, by force of circumstances. With many, let us hope with most, their only blame was that attaching to a simplicity which allowed itself to be gulled in the hope of sharing sudden gain, wholly disproportionate to their investments. God, who makes our backslidings to correct us, will, we are sure, yet work some high and lasting good out of our calamities. O the 'uncertainty of riches'. O the unchanging love and care of God".[320]

Booth was not involved and it was quite a reasonable decision at that time for him to leave much of the money he had realized from the sale of his business with one of the Melbourne banks and to arrange for drafts to be sent to Blantyre regularly. Late in 1892 these drafts became less reliable and then stopped completely.[321]

The collapse of the Melbourne banks of issue

The collapse of the land boom resulted in much fraud being brought into the open, and one financial institution, the Premier Permanent Building Association, had already collapsed earlier (20.12.1889). But it was only one, and in its case fraud had played a major role.[322] As the economic situation deteriorated in 1892, the whole Australian banking system came under pressure, and a number of factors combined to bring about the most severe economic crisis Australia had ever gone through, and the former boom city Melbourne was hit the hardest.[323]

---

[320] *The Victorian Freeman*, Feb 1889, p. 22.

[321] Harry Langworthy, *The Life of Joseph Booth*, pp. 36-37.

[322] E.A. Boehm, *Prosperity and Depression in Australia 1887-1897*, Oxford: Clarendon, 1971, p. 260.

[323] Books on the bank failures and their context are: E.A. Boehm, *Prosperity and Depression in Australia 1887-1897*, Oxford: Clarendon, 1971; A.R. Hall, *The Stock Exchange of Melbourne and the Victorian Economy 1852-1900*, Canberra: Australian National University Press, 1968; N.G. Butlin, *Investment in Australian Economic Development 1861-1900*, Cambridge University Press, 1964.

In 1892 the Australian colonies were still eight years away from federation and central government, let alone a federal reserve bank. Even Victoria did not have such a thing, with a number of private "banks of issue" sharing in the job of issuing the necessary currency. Some of these operated only in Victoria, some in more than one colony, and some were subsidiaries of British banks. These banks were supplied with the necessary capital from local savings and from loans raised in Britain.[324]

As it was usual in those days, banks could lend out a higher percentage of the money deposited with them than today in Europe, so they were more likely to suffer from withdrawals caused by an economic downturn. Due to the collapse of the land boom an increasing number had to liquidate their savings and many who had taken up credit, secured by land as collateral, defaulted in repayment and the banks could not recover their loans because it had become practically impossible to sell land, or if so, only at extremely low prices.

This situation was exacerbated by the discovery not only of light-hearted financial management, but also of outright fraud, much of it committed after the land boom collapsed, ostensibly to keep the banks from collapsing as well.

In their earlier days, good and strong, the banks had offered depositors of fixed deposits the option of withdrawing their deposit any time before maturity at the price of forfeiting all interest accrued so far. What had brought the banks profit in good days brought them down in lean days as money invested could be withdrawn at will.

Psychology played its role, too. When it became obvious that there were liquidity problems in a bank, a run on the bank's dwindling deposits could start and finally bring the bank down, so that it had to close, hopefully to reopen after "restructuring."

The banking crisis, which had been looming for quite some time, became obvious when a run on the Imperial Banking Company started, which forced it to suspend business on 24.7.1891. Those who had withdrawn their money early in the run were the lucky ones, the others had their savings tied up for a long time or would even lose them partly or completely. In Melbourne alone 21 financial institutions connected

---

[324] Since Victoria was booming, these loans were easy to raise and often oversubscribed: "The third instalment of the Victorian loan for £ 8,000,000 floated in London at an average of £ 108 13s 10d. There were 270 tenders for £ 3,460,00, the amount required being £ 1,500,000. The price obtained was £ 4 13s 10d above the minimum fixed" ("Notable Events" 10.1.1888).

to the land boom collapsed,[325] and that brought down many of the Melbourne banks and created a banking crisis affecting all of Australia.[326]

The Booths had done their business under good economic circumstances, and since Joseph Booth sold his share in the ice parlour early in 1891, the collapse of the financial institutes related to the land boom did not affect him yet. So it was quite proper for him to put the proceeds of the sale into a bank and to arrange for regular transfers of money to wherever he would go.

I was not able to find out with which bank Booth had deposited his money, but since the majority of the banks crashed, one can hardly accuse Booth of making a wrong choice. The banks were all among the top banks in Australia. Their cash flow problems account for the fact that at first the drafts became irregular[327] and the crash accounts for the end of the transfers, at least for a longer period.

Booth and the Melbourne crisis

In 1893 Booth, trusting that his own money would come, had bought land[328] and employed labourers to develop coffee fields.[329] When money had failed to come in September 1892, Booth approached the Vice Consul at Blantyre for a small loan to tide him over. Alfred Sharpe was happy to refuse any assistance[330] and told Booth just to go home for good. It is interesting that the major critic of Booth among current historians is Robert Boeder,[331] who is a great admirer of Alfred Sharpe.[332]

Booth sold some of his belongings, and a loan which Captain R.C. Sclater, an engineer working for Sharpe's administration, offered him,

---

[325] E.A. Boehm, *Prosperity and Depression*, p. 264. Only the Land Mortgage Bank of Victoria, the oldest of them all, did not collapse.

[326] Out of 22 Australian banks, one was liquidated (Federal Bank of Australia, Head Office in Melbourne) and 12 suspended operations and reopened after a period of "restructuring" of between 31 and 130 days. Of the nine banks that did not suspend operations, only the Royal Bank of Australia had its headquarters in Melbourne (E. A. Boehm, *Prosperity and Depression,* p. 272).

[327] Cf. Harry Langworthy, *The Life of Joseph Booth*, pp. 36-37

[328] For the circumstances see: Harry Langworthy, *The Life of Joseph Booth*, 35-37.

[329] A good number of them were slaves from Ngoniland, sent by their owners under a contract which would allow them to purchase their freedom through the income to their owners from work at Mitsidi. Cf. Langworthy, *The Life of Joseph Booth*, p. 37.

[330] Harry Langworthy, *The Life of Joseph Booth*, p. 36.

[331] Robert B. Boeder, "Reassessing Joseph Booth", *Kleio* (Pretoria), July 1983, p. 14.

[332] Robert B. Boeder, *Alfred Sharpe of Nyasaland. Builder of Empire*, Blantyre: Society of Malawi, 1981.

greatly helped to tide him over until money from Britain arrived in November 1892.[333]

The closure of the banks had the immediate effect that needed money was tied up for an indefinite period, like in the case of the Victorian Baptists' foreign mission money for India. As such missions were relying on regular giving of the faithful, they would not have much capital in a bank. Booth was in a different situation, having sold his business and having deposited all the money with a bank. Since he had managed to attract considerable support in Britain, for Mitsidi the crisis was temporary and since most banks reopened after "restructuring", this would mean that not all was lost and that he would recover a good part of his money after some time.[334]

More than Booth's work it was the work at Likhubula (Nyasa Industrial Mission) that was hit by Melbourne's financial crisis. When Booth had been given a chance to publicize his intended industrial mission work in the *Victorian Baptist*, the editor applauded and endorsed the idea, but also pointed out:

> Our one difficulty in responding just now in responding to Mr. Booth's touching appeal is the depleted condition of our exchequer. One frets to think of all that might have been done, had we as a community possessed the spirit of combined prudence and liberality. Would that some of the vanished millions were in use in the great and glorious work of evangelizing the heathen! However, all we can do is to hope that the provisional committee of Mr. Booth's mission may find a generous response to their appeal, and that, without interfering with existing obligations.[335]

Obviously some extra money was found, as personnel from Victoria was sent indeed to develop Likhubula as an Australian Mission station, with Booth paying for it from his own funds.[336]

In August 1893 Oliver Deeath, his wife and Frank Miller came, followed soon by Miss Dawes and Mr. Martin.[337] William Lucas, a member of Brighton Baptist and the secretary of the Preachers' Society there,

---

[333] Harry Langworthy, *The Life of Joseph Booth*, p. 37.
[334] There is no direct information yet available to me on this time. But I make the assumption on the grounds that all but one of the banks reopened.
[335] *The Victorian Baptist*, 11/1892, p. 204.
[336] This makes it look likely that the financial crisis of September and October 1892 was not due to the collapse of his bank but due to cash flow problems of that bank leading to the collapse in 1893.
[337] Harry Langworthy, *The Life of Joseph Booth*, p. 69.

travelled to Malawi to see the new work there.[338] Booth soon ran into trouble when his Australian supporters, under pressure from Blantyre Mission, abandoned him. He was especially hurt that Rev Howard, pastor of Brighton Baptist Church and now secretary of the Australian Auxiliary, also abandoned him.[339]

Sufficient sources are not yet available, but maybe it was not just freshly found respect for mission comity that made him a more than reluctant supporter, but also the economic realities of Melbourne, which by 1894 was in a recession as deep as the boom had been high.

Booth tried to adjust to the new realities. At the end of 1894, his connection to the Zambezi Industrial Mission had been severed, but he continued to legally own the Likhubula estate and decided to both separate it from ZIM and to find new support for it, not in depressed Australia but in Britain. The English Baptist Missionary Society refused to accept new responsibilities, but he found support among his old associates connected to the East London Training Institute of Fanny and Grattan Guinness. The initial support that led to the formation of the Nyasa Industrial Mission, came from three Baptists, all three of them closely related to Spurgeon's Tabernacle (Richard Cory, John P. Clerk, Alfred Tilly), and at least two of them (Cory and Tilly) had been involved in early faith missions. Tilly and Cory had been major supporters of Fanny Guinness' Livingstone Inland Mission,[340] the second faith mission after the China Inland Mission and the first faith mission in Africa.[341] Richard Cory had also been a Zambesi Industrial Mission trustee and was Nyasa Industrial Mission president from 1894 until his

---

[338] The Victorian Baptist 7/1893, p. 148. As a result of his journey he published: William Lucas, "A Band of African Girls" (*The Victorian Baptist*, July 1894) about Njawa, Ndapeuli, Chesoyaga, Iwasaneya, Meli, and Ngatwaika, asking the readers to pray for them.

[339] Harry Langworthy, The Life of Joseph Booth, pp. 59-60.

[340] Rev Alfred Tilly of Cardiff was the first secretary of the Livingstone Inland Mission in Congo (1878-1880) before Fanny Guinness took over. Cory was a Baptist layman, also from Cardiff.

[341] It was started in 1878 with the aim of establishing a chain of mission stations to reach the interior of Congo from the mouth of the Congo River. A chain of missions were established to get around the rapids, then one at Kinshasa. A steamer was put on the river, and Equator mission was opened upstream. In 1884 Fanny Guinness handed the mission over to the American Baptist Foreign Missionary Union, led by Adoniram Judson Gordon, a leading personality of the American Holiness Revival (Fanny Guinness, "Transfer of the Congo Mission", *The Word, the Work and the World*, 1884, pp. 148-150) in the (mistaken) hope that this mission would be able to pursue a vigorous expansion into the interior, especially using black American missionaries (Klaus Fiedler, Ganz auf Vertrauen. Geschichte und Kirchenverständnis de Glaubensmissionen, Gießen/Basel, 1992, p. 115.

death in 1914.[342] Thus the economic depression, combined with more personal factors, made Likhubula, the mission station founded by Booth for the Australians, to become the nucleus of a new British faith mission,[343] while some Australians continued to serve with ZIM, centred on Mitsidi.

8. Booth and Australia

The Australian period of Booth did not last long, just about four years,[344] but it was an important one, and Booth also influenced the world of Australian Protestant missions.

Whereas the Auckland period had formed Joseph Booth's spiritually, the years in Melbourne were formative for Booth as a missionary. His missionary work did not start in Africa, but in Melbourne as a member of Brighton Baptist Church, when he introduced the "Young Men's Mutual Improvement Society" and when he became a street evangelist on Queen's Wharf and a missionary to the Secularists.

In Melbourne he must also have developed his innovative Industrial Mission approach. When Booth left for England in 1891 to explore the possibilities, he had already a clear concept of industrial missions in mind, as his conversation with the BMS secretary shows,[345] and the Booths had already sold the business for that purpose. In London Booth based his arguments on William Carey,[346] but there is so far no detailed evidence how Booth had learned about the industrial mission idea. One reasonable idea is that, since he regularly read the *Missionary Review of the World*, which was spiritually close to the Holiness Movement and the faith missions, and which regularly and approvingly reported on William Taylor's self-supporting missions, that

---

[342] Henry Smith (ed.), *The Jubilee of the Nyasa Mission 1893-1943*, Cowley, 1943.

[343] *Ibid.*, p. 14.

[344] But then it must be kept in mind that hardly any period in Booth's life lasted long.

[345] Langworthy reports the Secretary to have spoken like this, quoting the SDA *Review and Herald* of 13.5.1902: "We do not know any Carey in this day. We have no Carey and if you want that kind of work, you would better go and do it. If you want a missionary society of that kind, you will have to found one (Harry Langworthy, *The Life of Joseph Booth*, p. 24).

[346] For Carey's theology see: Thomas Schirrmacher, *Postmillennialism and the Theology of World Missions*, Bonn: VKW, 1992.

he was influenced from that side.[347] In 1892 he published his plan in the *Missionary Review of the World*.[348]

Booth did not invent the idea of self-supporting Industrial Missions, but in his surroundings, this was a new idea, and the Booths had applied it very clearly to their own property, making the proceeds from the sale the financial nucleus of their industrial mission venture.

Australia and Booth

The late 1880s, when the Booths lived in Brighton, were the period in which the Australian Faith Mission Movement was born. There, as elsewhere, it was headed by the CIM, with Mary Reed of Launceston, Tasmania as the first missionary. However, she sailed in 1888 from England. In 1899, four Melbourne men, one of them a Baptist,[349] started a regular prayer meeting, which led to Parsons becoming the first Victorian CIM missionary in May 1890. In the same year Mary Reed, back from China due to ill health, caused a major wave of support for the CIM that led to the birth of the Australian Council of the CIM, which held its first meeting on 21.5.1890 in a room at Collins Street Baptist Church, the mother church of all Baptist churches in Victoria.[350]

All this led in turn to Hudson Taylor's visit to Australia. A great farewell meeting was held in Melbourne Town Hall on 27.10.1890, just opposite Booth's Milk Palace, with 3000 in attendance.[351] Therefore it is not astonishing that the messenger, calling Mrs Booth in her dream to become a missionary, was a Chinese, and it is no wonder either that Joseph Booth, while in London, explored the possibility to serve with the CIM.[352] What new thing, then, did Booth give to the Australian Missionary Movement? He was, to my knowledge, the first to apply the

---

[347] *The Victorian Freeman* also reported regularly on Bishop William Taylor ("who has many friends in Australia"), July 1888. On Bishop Taylor see also: Klaus Fiedler, *The Story of Faith Missions, p. 53f.*

[348] Joseph Booth, "The Greatest Work in the World", *Missionary Review of the World*, 5 (Aug. 1892), pp. 573-580. Cf. Harry Langworthy, *The Life of Joseph Booth*, pp. 26-28.

[349] The Anglicans H.B. Macartney and H. Parsons of Caulfuld, the Presbyterian W.L. Morton and the Baptist Alfred Bird (Marcus L. Loane, *The Story of the CIM in Australia 1890-1964*, Melbourne 1965).

[350] *Ibid.*, pp. 6-7

[351] *Ibid.*, p. 11.

[352] Booth seems not to have applied to the Australian Council, which would have been the regular thing to do, since the Booths lived in Melbourne and the Council had its office there, too, in Collins Street Baptist Church. It is quite possible that Booth knew that with his industrial mission idea he would not fit into the CIM.

industrial mission idea in Australia and the first to direct Australian missionary interests to Africa in general and to Malawi in particular, thus
starting a relationship, which continues to this day.

The Greatest Work in the World - A Plea for Missionary Enterprise[353]

By Joseph Booth

[The writer of this article has a right to be heard, for he has started for Africa to carry out in person his own convictions. -Ed]

The following statements and suggestions are addressed to believers in the Lord Jesus Christ who accept His words as final, who rejoice in Him as their Saviour, and expect shortly to stand before Him as their Judge.

The "greatest work in the world" is that marked out by the Lord Jesus Christ to be accomplished by His followers between His ascension and His return - viz., this Gospel of the kingdom shall be preached in the whole world for a testimony unto all the nations; and then shall the end come (Matt. 24:14); and again more definitely after the resurrection His last words were, "All authority hath been given me in heaven and on earth; go ye, therefore, and make disciples of all the nations, ... and lo, I am with you always, even unto the end of the world."

We have heard these solemn and definite words so frequently that they have become trite and almost powerless. We do not recognize in them an utterance of the mightiest possible significance to every kindred, tribe, and tongue; compassing a work so large that after eighteen centuries it is far from complete; an utterance, indeed, that may yet have power to rise up in judgment against us.

Gazed at in the light of the great white throne, what do the words mean to present-day Christians? Simply this, that if the trust is not yet discharged it is for us, the Christians of this generation, to rise up at once in the strength of the Lord and with loving obedience carry out His great parting command.

Is the work done? No. Eight hundred millions of our fellow-travelers to eternity have never heard of Christ or of heaven.

What is being done? Between seven and eight thousand European missionaries are now in the field, and about three million pounds yearly are subscribed for the work.

Can these overtake the work? No; for there still remains eight hundred millions of heathen whom they cannot reach.

Are more labourers willing to go? Yes; over six thousand in America alone are waiting, and probably over several thousand more in Great Britain and her colonies.

Why are they not sent? Because funds are not available, the revenue of almost every society, as shown by the annual reports, being already overtaxed, and some having large deficits.

---

[353] *The Missionary Review of the World*, January to December 1892, pp. 573-580.

What is needed to complete the work and give the "Bread of Life" to all? In order to give one messenger to every twenty thousand heathen forthwith, forty thousand more workers would be required.

Have the believers in Christ sufficient men and means to send the required members?

Yes; probably so.

Then why is it not done? Ah! It is not for us to judge one another. The great day will declare whether *we* have done *our* part.

Is there any solution of the difficulty? There must be, since Christ has "all power," and He says, "Go," and because He guarantees His presence to the end of time.

That we have a right to expect and demand in God's name that every barrier shall give way is manifest from such promises as Isa. 41:10; 45:2, 3, 6; 54:2-4; 60:1-5. There may be many ways of attaining the desired end, but is not one solution found in the principle laid down by Carey (the father of modern missions) a century ago - viz., that each mission station be made self-supporting and self-propagating?

May not the work of the future need to be done where possible on these lines?

Since the work of Carey and his two compeers resulted in their earning over £61,000 and expending the same on mission work in India, planting twenty-six native churches, translating the Bible wholly or in part into thirty-four languages besides supporting themselves in comfort, the practicability and great possibilities of the method is demonstrated.

That they may not have been ordinary men is probable; but who is ordinary that takes full hold of the mighty power at command stored up in the "exceeding great and precious promises," which are all "yea and amen in Christ Jesus, unto the glory of God by us"?

That great natural gifts, though desirable, are not essential is manifest from such assurances as Luke 10:21; 1 Cor. 1:26-28.

Let us review the position for a moment:

The work to be done is plain; "the field is the world."

The advance guard of workers are waiting with untold reserves to follow.

God's purpose is plain, "I will give Thee for a Light unto the Gentiles, that Thou mayest be My salvation unto the ends of the earth."

The barriers to the Gospel are down or falling on every hand.

The Christians of this generation have the knowledge, the men, the means, and the responsibility.

The power of God to do the work is at our disposal.

All needed elements are, therefore, at our command to do the work, if we have the will to apply them.

Who will avail themselves of the high calling of God?

Who, with humble thankfulness to Him for being permitted to become co-workers with God in earth's noblest and greatest work, part of His eternal plan

(John 3:16), the theme of heaven (Luke 15:7) and the joy of eternity (Rev 5:9-13), will throw their whole being, body, soul, spirit, experience, and means into this glorious work?

Who will count it higher than earth's highest honor to be the ambassadors from God to those whom He expressly designs shall hear His message?

Who is willing to bury this own little will and live only to do the great will of God?

Who is willing to hear the Lord say, "As My Father sent me, even so send I you"? and again, "I will make you fishers of men"? and yet again, "Ye have not chosen Me, but I have chosen you and ordained you, that ye should go and bring forth fruit"? (John 15:16.)

Who with a holy, heaven-born resolve will determine "that neither things present nor things to come" shall prevent them from taking the part God would have them take in this great work?

Let us remember that the blood of over fifty thousand heathen, dying daily without the knowledge of God, will rest upon this generation if we neglect to rise with a mighty purpose to the work He has given us the privilege and responsibility of doing. (Read Prov. 24:11, 12; Ezek. 3:18.)

Let us look with unaverted gaze at our Lord's searching words, "He that receiveth not My sayings, the word I have spoken, the same shall judge him in the last day;" again, "Fear not them that kill the body;" "He that loveth his life shall lose it; and he that loseth his life for My sake shall find it;" again, "Sell all thou hast, ... and come follow Me;" "Whosoever doth not bear his cross and come after Me cannot be My disciple;" again, "Every one that hath forsaken houses, or brethren, or sisters, or father, or mother, or wife, or children, or lands for My name's sake, shall receive an hundred-fold and shall inherit eternal life" (Matt. 19:29).

The position of the present-day believer is accurately expressed in the words of the late Hon. Keith Falconer: "While vast continents are shrouded in almost utter darkness, and hundreds of millions suffer the horrors of heathenism, the burden of proof lies upon you to show that the circumstances in which God has placed you were meant by Him to keep you *out* of the mission field."

Beware of consulting flesh and blood too much; consult Jesus Christ.

Beware of the wiles of Satan to lull to sleep and apathy.

Beware of the evasive suggestions of our own hearts, since the Word of God declares "the heart is deceitful above all things."

Beware of laying too much stress on education or any human qualification. Resolve to obey or yield up life in the attempt, and God will open the way to such education as is needed.

Beware of losing the place God would have you fill in His great eternal purposes.

Beware of leaning unduly upon earthly props, which may fail you at the critical moment; lean lightly upon the human, heavily on the Divine.

Beware of that false humility which says, "I can do nothing," and forgets that God engages to use "the weak things, and things which are not," "to bring to nought the things which are."

Beware of expecting too much from the wise, the mighty, the noble, or the rich, knowing that they have their special hindrances and temptations.

Beware of finding fault with others or dwelling upon what they might do.

Beware of drinking at human fountains, but take deep draughts at the Fountain-head.

"Quench not the spirit."

Believing that the needed workers will be forthcoming when the requirements of God are faithfully displayed and calmly considered, how shall the means of support be provided?

> I. As far as may be by the subscriptions of those whose hearts are in the work and sympathize with the method proposed, but cannot from various causes go themselves.

> II. By planting industrial missions on the principle alluded to - viz., to become "self-supporting and self-propagating."

How would such missions affect the problem? Assuming that each worker be helped for a period not exceeding the first two years, in the course of fifty years the same yearly income would put twenty-five times the volume of workers in the field; in the course of a century fifty times the number of workers as compared with the permanently supported laborers.

Doubtless both types, "the sustained and self-sustaining," will be found necessary according to the ground worked and the habits or capacities of the workers.

While "industrial missions" may be harder to plant and permanently consolidate, it must be borne in mind this method opens the door to bring into the work the reserve forces of the rank and file of Christian workers, who are used to the task of toiling at various occupations and handicrafts.

The Apostle Paul, who knew something of the work to be done, approved and adopted this method for the missionary's work of breaking up fallow ground, and continued it during the early stages of church life, as recorded in 2 Thess. 3:8, 9; 1 Cor. 3:11, 12.

Has not the special time come for Christian workingmen to come forward and give their working powers to God and His great redemptive work? Farmers, artisans, engineers, miners, mechanics, and tradesmen, who, while supporting themselves, proclaim the Gospel in word and work.

Is not the workingman of the world the great wealth producer?

Have not the consecrated Christian workingmen of this generation one key in their hands to the great missionary problem, if ready and willing to use it?

Are they not able under God, and endued with the promised power from on high ("For the promise is to you and to your children, and to all that are afar off"), to rise up in one mighty crusade against heathendom, and so do a mighty work for God and humanity?

If this be so, does not the onus rest on the Christian workingmen of this generation to make use of the great power and responsibility attached to their position, especially if funds are forthcoming to tide over the initial difficulties for the first two years?

It is written, "The earth is the Lord's and the fulness thereof: the world and they that dwell therein." Is this a mere figure of speech, or is it a mighty eternal fact?

Mr Spurgeon says this title "ought to put the work of missions on a very cheering footing." Let us go and take possession in the name of the Lord.

Our Savior said, "The children of this world are wiser in their generation than the children of light." Certain it is that without a command from on high and without the Christian's title they take possession of the earth and its fullness, braving all dangers. Psalm 24:1 is the Christian's title to do this in the name of the rightful owner.

Take earth's darkest picture, cruel, bleeding, chaotic Africa, with its average of eight to ten thousand victims every day to slave-raiding, tyranny, and cannibalism. What is needed to transform that picture and to develop Africa's vast pastoral, agricultural, and mineral resources, and to rightly apply the earth's fullness God has stored there?

Is it to be the "children of this world" who, without society aids or a "Go ye," will presently take possession, fill their pockets, button them up, degrade the native, and make the missionary's work the harder?

Or shall it be what the British and American Christians are able to give and be the better for it -viz., some thousands of consecrated Christian workingmen?

A few Christian workers are resolved to commence work in Africa forthwith on the lines indicated. Two parties have left for the field within the last eight months, with the expectation of more to follow.

Africa is chosen because it presents two special features: First, it is the darkest picture of paganism on the earth. Its lawlessness, its tyranny of chiefs, its slave-raiding, its cannibalism, its never-ending inter-tribal wars, mark it as a most painful picture to the heart of Him "who came to seek and to save them that are lost;" and second, its resources are largely undeveloped and awaiting those who will take possession in God's name and for His work; at the same time training the native to develop his own country and take his rightful place in the universe.

The objects and aims of the mission are as follows, subject to such corrections or amendments as may be found conducive to the work as a whole:

(a) To plant industrial mission stations that shall become self-supporting within the first two years.

(b) The first base of operations to be in the territory of the British South African Chartered Company - viz., "on the Zambesi."

(c) To establish a prayer union throughout the British race, if possible, pledge to ask of God daily the speedy evangelization of the heathen throughout the world.

(d) To ask God to raise up an advocate or advocates to itinerate through the churches and Young Men's Christian Associations of Great Britain, America, Canada, and the colonies, soliciting men and means, and directing particular attention to the recommendation of our Lord, "Sell all thou hast, ... and come follow Me."

(e) Select and equip parties of two or three families or three to six young men, prepared to work as locality may require or their abilities enable them, at tilling the ground, food producing, grain growing, irrigating, seed or fruit growing and exporting, carpentering, blacksmithing, dairy farming, mining, printing, sheep farming, cattle rearing, and especially some light manufacture requiring small capital and suitable for native trained workers, easy of transport and export; all work to be combined with preaching and teaching, though all volunteers need not necessarily be speakers.

(f) Candidates to endeavour to become self-supporting from the very first or at the earliest possible moment, and further endeavour to provide funds or products with which to bring other laborers or to plant other stations farther afield.

(g) No missionary to trade or have any private undertaking on his own account; all property and increment to be vested in the mission trustees.

(h) The threefold type of workers - viz., the family type, the young man-celibate type and the sisterhood type, to be used according to locality and candidates.

(i) Female volunteers not to be expected to become self-supporting, but to be optional with them.

(j) Avail to be taken of the protection afforded by such chartered companies as the British South African and British East African, and grants of land to be sought promptly according to the advantages offered to aid or induce immigration and settlement, due regard being taken to suitableness of locality for Gospel work among the natives.

(k) Aim not only at the conversion of the natives, but at training and educating the young; forming new and industrious habits, taking them on stations to work side by side with white men, that they may realize "One is your Master, even Christ, and all ye are brethren." Specially aim at planting a simple form of Christian civilization transparent by contrast with paganism.

(l) Train and cultivate native converts' spiritual gifts, and lead to self-reliant action in preaching and planting industrial missions in the "regions beyond."

(m) When stations become supported by voluntary offerings of converts or congregations, the trading, farming, or manufacturing scaffolding to be either dispensed with or realized, transplanted or continued, as may be conducive to the progress of the whole work.

(n) Such churches not to become dependent of the mission, but to conduct their pastoral work at a moderate cost; the express purpose of the church's existence - viz., the diffusion of the Gospel of Christ among all peoples and throughout the whole earth, to be kept prominently in the foreground, and all surplus-giving power to be cultivated and directed into that channel.

(o) If suitable men are forthcoming, plant churches on the same basis in the existing towns in South Africa as opportunity occurs.

(p) Keep in regular and sympathetic touch by circular, periodical, or visitation with the churches and Young Men's Christian Associations, as far as opportunity is afforded, throughout Great Britain, America, Canada, and the colonies, furnishing the latest news from the front throughout the whole mission field, and offering to take suitable workers of proven Christian character with or without means, to be sent either at the Church's, the Association's, or the mission's expense, as may be found expedient; the purpose being to promote a healthy circulation from the centre to the circumference, and relieve the congestion in the more developed spheres of Christian labour, thus providing a legitimate outlet for the many one-talent Christians who too often stagnate in the home circle.

(q) The base of operations in each centre of work to be kept strong, and each outgoing branch well supported and fostered from its local centre.

(r) The ultimate object of the mission to be not only the overtaking of the work in Africa, but the training and equipping of messengers and the providing or earning adequate funds for the completion of the then unfinished work throughout the world; taking first in order the lands most suited to the needs of the system, in point of undeveloped resources or abundance of labour, as also the respective needs of the natives.

(s) In the early stages of the mission special care to be taken to secure good climatic and fair commercial, agricultural, or manufacturing conditions, as far as may be consistent with nearness of native population for mission work.

Finally, work as if all depended upon man; pray and trust, knowing all increase must come from God.

A Band of Central African Girls

By William Lucas.[354]

TRAVELLING along a pathway out in the rocky mountain side a few months ago on a bright, warm afternoon, I reached a mission house nestling in a delightful gorge that commands an extensive and beautiful panorama of African scenery. Recently I told the boys about some African dark-skinned lads I had met, and now I wish to confine my few words to a band of Central African girls, living far away inland from the East coast, beneath a mountain range that towers far above the Shire highlands, and looks down upon the chain of great inland lakes. I must confess that I feel interested in these girls, and should like all Victorian girls to feel even more so.

Njawa was for a time residing on the mission station where I was a guest, but her mother for some time past has refused to let her do so; and another, Ndapeuli, who was an old scholar and would like to learn more, is, unfortunately for her, such a good gardener that the people in the village say:—"If Ndapeuli goes who goes who will help us to hoe?" Now, I want you to pray for these two girls, that they may not be deprived of the Christian privileges within their reach, but that God will turn the mothers' and the villagers' hearts to allow them to share in that they have learnt to love.

Then there are two girls, Chesoyaga, whose progress is very satisfactory, and her influence especially good on the younger girls, and Iwasaneya, a particularly gentle and amiable girl, the chief assistant in the sewing class; each possessed of simple faith that I am sure some will especially give thanks for as well as uphold in prayer. They are taking a firm stand against certain most objectionable native ceremonies, the refusal to join in which means a great deal to them, far more of disgrace and shame than we living in Christian lands can understand.

But, as you know, even girls vary; and mission work among African girls has its pleasures and disappointments. While some are a source of comfort and delight to the missionaries, others give trouble. Ngatwaika is one of the troublesome class; though preferring to be in the company of those at the station, seemed never to be at ease. Given to fits of temper, and occasionally running away, it was felt that her influence was not being for good on the other girls. So it was thought

---

[354] *The Victorian Baptist,* July 1894. I have included this article with the hope that some of the names can be identified here in Malawi.

best for her to live in the village near by at least for a time, and to let her come and do laundry work instead of being resident at the station. A little earnest prayer on her behalf I am sure would do no harm. God can influence hearts in Africa, even those that are bad tempered, and make thoughtless girls steady and attentive to that which is for their highest good.

Then I should like you remember at the Throne of Grace Meli and her friend, whose name I forget. They rendered me many a helpful service on another mission station, and are proving of great assistance to God's servants there. Ah! God only knows what is in store for these and many other girls that I have met in the dark continent, simply clad in bark cloth, or two or three yards of calico twined round their bodies, hatless and bootless, with a simple bead necklace, a few twists of brass wire on their arm, and a grass comb stuck in their hair. Knowing almost nothing of our modes of living, and having few wants, until quite recently they lived in their native villages, gossiped, lounged about, knew nothing of reading, writing, sewing, or household duties. Idled their time away except for a few weeks that they hoed in the fields.

A band of African girls! Why not put their names on a card or in a birthday book so as not to forget them? Njawa, Ndapeuli, Chesoyaga, Iwasaneya, Meli, Ngatwaika are truly worthy of our remembrance.

Bibliography

A Short History of Africa Evangelical Fellowship in Malawi from 1900 to 1989, np., nd., 3 pp. (copy at the Baptist Theological Seminary, Lilongwe).

A Sunday School's Half-Century 1858-1908, Baptist Tabernacle, Auckland, New Zealand, Auckland: 1908, 38 pp, richly illustrated.

"Auckland", *World Book Millennium 2000*, International Standard English Edition, Version 4.0, IBM, CD ROM).

Baptist Church Wellesley St., Auckland, *Manual*, Auckland, 1878.

Barr, John, *The City of Auckland, New Zealand, 1840-1920*, Auckland et al: Whitcombe and Tombs, 1922.

Boeder, Robert B., "Reassessing Joseph Booth", *Kleio* (Pretoria), July 1983. .

Boeder, Robert B., *Alfred Sharpe of Nyasaland. Builder of Empire*, Blantyre: Society of Malawi, 1981.

Boehm, E.A., *Prosperity and Depression in Australia 1887-1897*, Oxford: Clarendon, 1971.

Booth, Catherine, *Female Ministry. Woman's Right to Preach the Gospel*, London: Morgan & Chase, nd.

Booth, Joseph, "The Author's Apology", in Joseph Booth (Laura Perry [ed.]), *Africa for the African*, Blantyre: CLAIM-Kachere, [3]1998(1897), p. 73-74.

Booth, Joseph, "The Greatest Work of the World - A Plea for Missionary Enterprise", *Missionary Review of the World* 1892, pp. 573-580).

Booth, Joseph, *Africa for the African*, Baltimore: Morgan College Press, [1]1897, [2]1897; reprinted Blantyre: CLAIM-Kachere, 1998 (ed. Laura Perry) and Zomba: Kachere, 2008.

Booth-Langworthy, Emily, *This Africa was Mine*, Stirling: Sterling Tract Enterprises, 1950.

Brighton Baptist Church, *Annual Report*, 1889.

Broomhall, A.J., *Survivors' Pact*, London: Hodder and Stoughton and Overseas Missionary Fellowship, 1984.

Bush, G.W.A., *Decently and in Order. The Centennial History of the Auckland City Council*, Auckland/London: Collins, 1971.

Butlin, N.G., *Investment in Australian Economic Development 1861-1900*, Cambridge University Press, 1964.

Campbell, R.J., "'The Black Eighties' – Unemployment in New Zealand in the 1880s", *Australian Economic History Review*, xvi, pp. 67-82.

Carey, William, *An Enquiry into the Obligations of Christians to Use Means for the Conversion of the Heathens. In which the religious state of the different nations of the world, the success of former undertakings and the practicability of further undertakings, are considered*, Leicester 1792, pp. 13 and 52).

Compton's Interactive Encyclopedia, Cambridge, MA: The Learning Company, 1998.

Dahlitz, Ray, *Secular Who's Who. A Bibliographical Directory of Freethinkers, Secularists, Rationalists, Humanists, and others involved in Australia's Secular Movement from 1850 onwards*, Melbourne: nd.

Dann, Robert Bernard, *The Primitivist Missiology of Anthony Norris Groves: A Radical Influence on Nineteenth-Century Protestant Mission*, Victoria, BC: Trafford, 2007.

Day, Rendell, *From Gowa Industrial Mission to Landmark Missionary Baptists: One Hundred Years of Baptist Churches in Malawi, 1894-1994*, Zomba: Kachere, 2008 (Kachere Documents no. 52).

Devonport District School Centennial Publication 1870-1970, nd., np.

Dieter, Melvin, *The Holiness Revival of the Nineteenth Century*, Metuchen: Scarecrow 1980.

Domingo, Charles, *Letters of Charles Domingo*, ed. Harry Langworthy, Zomba: University of Malawi, Sources for the Study of Religion in Malawi no. 9, 1983.

Easton, B., "Three New Zealand Depressions", in W.E. Willmot (ed.), *New Zealand and the World: Essays in Honour of Wolfgang Rosenberg*, Christchurch: University of Canterbury, 1980.

Fessenden, David E., *Father to Nobody's Children: The Life of Thomas J. Barnardo*, Halesowen: Christian Literature Crusade, 1995.

Fiedler, Klaus, "Aspects of the Early History of the Bible School Movement", in Festschrift Donald Mooreland, ed. by Marthinus W. Praetorius: *The Secret of Faith. In Your Heart - In Your Mouth*, Heverlee/Leuven 1992, pp. 62-77.

Fiedler, Klaus, "Shifts in Eschatology - Shifts in Missiology", in: Jochen Eber (ed.), *Hope does not disappoint. Studies in Eschatology. Essays from Different Contexts*, Wheaton: World Evangelical Fellowship – Theological Commission, Bangalore: Theological Book Trust, 2001.

Fiedler, Klaus, "Joseph Booth and the Writing of Malawian History. An Attempt at Interpretation" *Religion in Malawi*, no. 6, 1996, pp. 30-38.

Fiedler, Klaus, *Ganz auf Vertrauen. Geschichte und Kirchenverständnis der Glaubensmissionen*, Gießen/Basel, 1992.

Fiedler, Klaus, *The Story of Faith Missions. From Hudson Taylor to Present Day Africa*, Oxford/Akropong/Buenos Aires, Irvine, New Delhi: Regnum Books International, ²1995(1994).

Klaus Fiedler, *Conflicted Power in Malawian Christianity: Essays Missionary and Evangelical from Malawi*, Mzuzu: Mzuni Press, 2015

Gray, Ernest, *The Early History of the Church of Christ Missionary Work in Nyasaland, Central Africa, 1907-1930*, Church of Christ Historical Society Occasional Paper No. 1 [Cambridge, 1981].

Guinness, Fanny, "Transfer of the Congo Mission", *The Word, the Work and the World*, 1884, pp. 148-150.

Guinness, Fanny, *The New World of Central Africa. With a History of the First Christian Mission on the Congo*, London 1890.

Guinness, Grattan, *Light for the Last Days. A Study Historical and Prophetical*, London 1886; ²1917.

Guinness, Lucy, *Only a Factory Girl*, London, 1886.

Guinness, Michelle, *The Guinness Legend*, London/Sydney/Auckland/Toronto: Hodder and Stoughton, 1990.

Hall, A.R., *The Stock Exchange of Melbourne and the Victorian Economy 1852-1900*, Canberra: Australian National University Press, 1968.

Hattaway, Robert and Margaret Willis, *When all the Saints. Celebrating 150 Years of All Saints' Church – Howick*, Auckland: Howick Parish, 1997.

Hawke, R., *The Making of New Zealand. An Economic History*, Cambridge University Press, 1985.

Hayes, Jeff, *Religion in Third World Politics*, Oxford: Blackwell, 1994.

Hill, Thomas F., "History of the Auckland Bapt. Tabernacle", *The Reaper*, 1924-26, p. 15.

Horridge, Glenn K., *the Salvation Army: Origins and Early Days: 1865-1900*. Godalming: Ammonite Books, 1993.

Hunt, Graeme, *The Rich List. Wealth and Enterprise in New Zealand 1820-2000*, Auckland: Reed, 2000.

Jones, Charles Edwin, *A Guide to the Study of the Holiness Movement*, Metuchen: Scarecrow 1974.

Langworthy, Harry, *'Africa for the African'. The Life of Joseph Booth*, Blantyre: CLAIM-Kachere, 1996.

Links with the Past. The Centenary of Brighton Baptist Church 1851-1951, Melbourne: 1951.

Loane, Marcus L. *The Story of the CIM in Australia 1890-1964*, Auckland, Melbourne: CIM/OMF, 1965.

Lucas, William, "A Band of African Girls", *The Victorian Baptist*, July 1894.

Makondesa, Patrick, *The Church History of Providence Industrial Mission*, Zomba: Kachere, 2006.

Müller, George, *A Narrative of some of the Lord's Dealings with George Müller Written by Himself*, London, [9]1895 ([1]1837).

Murray, Iain, *The Forgotten Spurgeon*, London 1966.

Musgrove, S. (ed.), *The Hundred of Devonport. A Centennial History*, Devonport: Borough Council, nd.

"Notable Events", *The Age Annual*, 1874-1876, 1879-1880, 1882-1890").

Page, George E., *A.G.B., The Story of the Life and Work of Archibald Geikie Brown*, London 1944.

Pastor Charles Bonongwe. Chosen, Called and Faithful, nd.

Philafrican Liberators' League (ed.), "The First Expedition Successful", New York, 1897 in Alida Chatelin (ed.), *Les rapports de la Mission Philafricain 1898-1905*, Lausanne, nd.

Phiri, D.D., *Let us Die for Africa*, Blantyre: 2000.

Phiri, D.D., *Let us Fight for Africa*, Zomba: Kachere, 2007.

Pierson, Arthur T., *The Keswick Movement in Precept and Practice*, New York/London 1903.

Pollock, John, *The Keswick Story - The Authorized History of the Keswick Convention*, Chicago: Moody, 1964.

Sanford, Don A., *A Choosing People: The History of Seventh Day Baptists*, Nashville: Broadman, 1992.

Schirrmacher, Thomas, *Postmillennialism and the Theology of World Missions*, Bonn: VKW, 1992.

Selby and Symes Debate. A Full Report of the Six Nights' Debate held in the Temperance Hall, Melbourne, in the months of August and September, 1892 between Joseph Symes, President and Lecturer of the Australasian Secular Association and Isaac Selby, Christian Minister. Melbourne: The Austral Publishing Company, 1892.

Sharpe, Jacque and J. de Joswald, Devonport District School, Historic Committee Papers, 1882-1885.

Sheehan, Susan, "A Social and Demographic Study of Devonport, 1850-1920," MA, University of Auckland, 1980.

Shelburne, C.B., *History of the Church of Christ in Malawi*, np., nd., 4 pp. (Copy at the Baptist Theological Seminary, Lilongwe).

Shepperson, George and Tom Price, *Independent African. John Chilembwe and the Nyasaland Rising of 1915*, Blantyre: CLAIM-Kachere [6]2000 (first edition Edinburgh University Press 1958).

Sinclair Keith, (ed.), *The Oxford Illustrated History of New Zealand*, Auckland: OUP, 1993 [1990].

Skinner, Craig, *Lamplighter and Son. The Forgotten Story of Thomas Spurgeon and his Famous Father, Charles Haddon Spurgeon*, Nashville: Broadman 1984.

Skinner, Craig, *Spurgeon and Son. The Forgotten Story of Thomas Spurgeon and his Famous Father, Charles Haddon Spurgeon*, Grand Rapids: Kregel, 1999.

Skinner, Ebenezer and J.G. Ross, "Sidney Jottings", *The Liberator* 1891, p. 2297.

Skinner, Ebenezer, *The Secularist's Guide. A Book for Young and Old*, Sydney, nd. [1890?].

Smith, Henry (ed.), *The Jubilee of the Nyasa Mission 1893-1943*, Cowley, 1943.

Spurgeon, Susannah and Joseph Harald (eds.), *C.H. Spurgeon. Autobiography, Compiled from his Diary, Letters and Records by his Wife and Private Secretary, London 1897-1910.* A two volume abbreviated version, London 1962 and 1973. .

Spurgeon, Thomas (ed.), *The Baptist Builder*, Published at the Auckland Tabernacle Bazaar, vol. 1, Dec. 1882.

Spurgeon, Thomas, *Auckland Tabernacle Opening Sermon*, (verbatim reported), Auckland: Theo Cooper, 1885, 18 pp.

Spurgeon, Thomas, *The Gospel of the Grace of God*, London: Passmore, 1883.

The Baptist Freeman, Oct 1889.

The Liberator 1887-1891.

The Melbourne Directory Sands and McDougall 1890.

The Melbourne Directory Sands and McDougall 1891.

The New Zealand Baptist.

The Victorian Baptist Witness, 5.9.1939.

The Victorian Baptist, 1890-1894.

The Victorian Freeman, 1888-1891.

The Zambezi Mission. Missionaries Support Themselves for Thirty Years, np, nd [1930].

Tomson, Paul, *A Handful of Grain. The Centenary History of the Baptist Union of New Zealand, vol. 1, 1851-1882*, Wellington, nd.

Walsh, T., *An Illustrated Story of Devonport and the Old North Shore 1841 to 1924, with an Outline of Maori Occupation to 1841*; Auckland, nd.

Wellesley Street Baptist Church, *Annual Report*, 1884.

Wilkin, F.J., *Baptists in Victoria. Our First Century 1838-1938*, Melbourne 1939.

Printed in the United States
By Bookmasters